D1409227

I am Magnetic

FEEL AND GROW RICH

DESIREE MANGANDOG, L.AC
ALONTO MANGANDOG, M.B.A.

ISBN 978-1-7327059-5-1

Edited by Rachel Gayle

Cover and Book Design by Rachel Gayle

Printed and bound in the United States of America
Peczuh Printing, Price, UT www.peczuh.com
First Printing September 2019

Published by Rhythm & Flow Project, LLC.
Spanaway, Washington 98387

Visit www.desireemangandog.com

To create a world of <u>*thriving artists...*</u>

Contents

CHAPTER 1: *Meet the Authors* ------------------------ 1

CHAPTER 2: *You are a Magnet* -------------------- 11

CHAPTER 3: *The Magnetic Framework* ----------- 25

CHAPTER 4: *The Road is Clear* ----------------- 39

CHAPTER 5: *Money Makeup* ---------------------- 69

CHAPTER 6: *Money and Me* ---------------------- 93

CHAPTER 7: *R + R: Release and Renew* ------- 103

CHAPTER 8: *Move to the Beat* ----------------- 123

CHAPTER 9: *I am Magnetic* --------------------- 143

APPLICATION POINT REFERENCES --------- 154

BIBLIOGRAPHY ------------------------------- 159

[CHAPTER 1]

Meet the Authors

Money.

A word that triggers a flood of emotion.

Zig Ziglar said it best: "Money isn't everything, but it sure ranks up there with oxygen."

It consumes a significant amount of attention within a 24-hour period. It certainly feels like oxygen, as our survival depends upon the ability to generate it.

Growing up, I found myself very interested in how adults made money. Why is it that certain people had the ability to create a lot of it easily, while others struggled to manage only a little? I was curious as to how it circulated throughout humanity. I wondered what made people decide to spend or invest it, and I was particularly interested in the sacrifices they continually made to earn it. I concluded that there must be a way to *learn* wealth creation. I decided that once I understood it, I would share it with others.

Even though I had a keen awareness and curiosity about money, I also found myself conflicted and confused about it. I cared more for spiritual matters and found myself rejecting the material world. I judged my mother for working so hard for the sake of money and the pursuit of status through material things. Looking back, I realize that I was naive then. Now that I have children, I understand the work ethic that is fueled with the desire to provide for their basic needs and opportunities.

Even so, as a child, I was concerned for my future self. How does an empathic, spiritual-seeker function in the "real world" and make a living? I discovered many artists and healers had a hard time creating high-level wealth. Most of them struggled to make ends meet. They would have to work an additional job to keep up. The idea of trading hours of your life for dollars seemed degrading and a kind of prison sentence that I wanted no part in.

I came to understand that it is a basic human right for a soul to live in its fullest expression. To not only have its basic needs met without worry, but to also have opportunities for self-discovery, spritual-growth, and to thrive. I wanted to encompass that and live it out. I have since made it my life's work: to live authentically as the spiritual-seeker and healer that I am while also creating a high-level income. My childhood desire to also teach others how is still a major priority in my life.

Sadly, I came to understand that not everyone wants to learn. We all have the opportunity for creativity and self-discovery while also having our needs met and exceeded, yet many still don't seek it. They don't want to know how they can change. Resistance to change is the greatest destructive force on this planet.

You, my dear soul friend, have picked up this book because you have found yourself ready for the change. You are in the 1% of the population who actively break-through resistance and dive into the unknown. Your checking account may not reflect it yet, but it will catch up.

Where attention goes, energy flows.

As you place your attention on improving your relationship with money, it is only inevitable for the dynamics to change.

It has been my obsession to improve my relationship with money and to master working with it in this life. This might sound superficial to some, but I promise you, it is much deeper than it seems.

In my opinion:

A person's relationship with money is a reflection of their mental, emotional and spiritual wellbeing.

It's a bold statement.

If you look at most individuals who have experienced financial success, you will notice similar qualities about them. It takes a great deal of clarity, mental and emotional maturity, persistance, patience, focus, trust, passion, service, courage and grit. Those who are stricken with self-doubt, pessimism, laziness, apathy, paralysis by fear, and a distrust of humanity consequently struggle in creating financial wellness.

Being that:

$$Emotions = Energy\ in\ Motion$$

This book uncovers the mental and emotional component for creating and managing money. My years of entrepreneurship has taught me that my thoughts and emotions play more of a significant role in wealth creation than actual strategies. Your habits of thinking and feeling influence everything. This book is about *being* rather than *doing*. Your *"being-ness"* affects your habits, behaviors, and circumstances that are called into your life. This is neither an accounting book nor a strategy book on wealth creation. Please make sure to consult with a trusted financial advisor, mentor, accountant and/or lawyer if you are seeking professional advice. Instead, this book is designed to transform your emotional relationship to money and heal the wounds that family and society have passed to us.

Prior to my entrepreneurial endeavors, the most money

I ever made as an adult was $2,000 in a month. I couldn't understand how people made even $5,000 in a month! At the age of 20, I often dreamt of becoming a millionaire. I was barely creating any income, yet I would read sales and marketing books. I watched my mother generate ridiculous wealth but would also witness it quickly slip through her fingers. I was determined to understand this *money game* that adults were often stressing about. I wanted to be different. I ached to be someone who was smart, responsible, and continually growing wealth. *But how?* Who could I learn from?

Not long after, my husband Alonto and I miraculously stumbled across our brilliant mentor, Rod Alan Richardson. *Thank you, YouTube!* He was looking for us and we were praying for him. Trust in life, my friend. When you ask for something, trust that it is on the way.

Rod was, and still is, the exact mentor we needed to show us how to transition from unnecessary struggle to life-giving freedom. It is truly a *mentor-student* match made in heaven. Rod taught us how to create and acknowledge the miracles all around us. The faith he held towards us became the bridge that crossed us into impacting thousands in their health journey. My hope is that Alonto and I can be one of your bridges, and help you cross over into a new version of yourself like Rod did for us.

Alonto and I have managed to double our income every year for the last five years. It's quite remarkable when we consider where we started from and compare it to the direction we are headed in today. We are still doing the necessary inner-work, just like you. Once you break through one layer of limitations, you'll find a new one. It's an ongoing growth process of meeting a challenge and conquering it in order to enter into your next level of awareness. It may sound like a lot of work, but it's also exciting to experience life in this way. Breaking through a money block liberates a soul to express its Divine genius. We want you to experience that! To truly feel *free*, not imprisoned by the lower vibrations most of humanity is plagued with. Personally, we don't see any better way to do this "life-thing". One *must* live in truth and love others immensely.

Even though our story is intricately woven together, Alonto also has stories that are uniquely his. To do them justice, we felt it was important for him to share in his own voice, which is captured in the alternate font on the next page and also throughout this book. So without further ado, I would love to introduce my my sweet, wise and gorgeous husband, *Alonto*.

This magical being is the love of my life and I am grateful that out of all of the women, he chose me. He may not ever say this in public, but I have the privilege of being the only woman he has ever said, "I love you" to. His parents disclosed that they were worried about Alonto, because he never had a love interest up until he brought me home to meet them at the age of 30. Believe me, *Asian parents worry a lot about these things.* 😂 Our little secret, though, okay? I'm not *too* confident that Alonto will read this, so I think it's safe that I shared. 😄

For the first 12 years of my life, I was raised in the Philippines. My father was an engineer and provided well-above the norm for our family. We had maids, cooks, nannies and a driver. Even though we were considered upper-middle-class, my mother still felt there was not enough opportunity for her children in our third-world country. She decided to make the sacrifice to move us to Michigan shortly after my 12th birthday. As a result, our family of five (me, my mom, and my three siblings) became first-generation immigrants.

The move was not the easiest thing on us, though. My mom had to work at Subway and Wendy's in order to provide for us. On such a limited income, we were forced to live in my aunt's basement. The five of us slept in a very small space for four years. Even with the dramatic change in lifestyle and the extreme poverty-driven money-mindset that my mother of us slept in a very small space for four years. Even with the dramatic change in lifestyle and the extreme poverty money-mindset that my mother holds onto to this day, I've managed to maintain an abundant view of money throughout my life.

I credit this to my uncle. He had a big part in raising and mentoring me before we moved to America. My uncle had a true entrepreneurial spirit and in turn, he cultivated the entrepreneur inside of me. What he cultivated never left.

At the age of eight, I had my first business endeavor. Even though I was still in the Philippines at the time, we had extended family in the US who would regularly mail us all kinds of American chocolates and candies. But I didn't really enjoy them and preferred the candies from my local area, instead. So, my uncle encouraged me to set up a candy stand. I sold those American chocolates for top dollar! Since my inventory was free, my business thrived! I loved every second of it.

At such an early age, money fascinated me. I quickly learned that money allowed you to buy the things you wanted. And as a kid, what I wanted was to go to the movies, buy my favorite chocolates, and play games. To me, making money looked like a game where the goal was to win by solving problems. And I discovered that I *loved* to win! Finding loopholes and shortcuts became my obsession.

The ironic thing is that the entrepreneurial side of me got stifled when coming to America. In Michigan, we were taught to work hard, get good grades in school, find a *safe* job, listen, and keep our heads down. American society seems to value security over taking risks. Thankfully, I decided to study abroad in Australia during my junior year of college for six months. My adventurous spirit returned on that trip, and I broke free from the *"money is hard to make"* mindset.

I've always been lucky in opportunities and money. The people around me have often lived in "lack", yet I always have the opposite experience. I would find myself asking, *"why me?"*. How did I get so many lucky breaks while others continued to suffer? Hence the decision to write this book. I subconsciously practiced key principles that contributed to the opportunities I've encountered. My intention for writing this, other than to satisfy the nudges from my beautiful wife, is to share those principles.

We live in a time where there is access to tremendous opportunity. Are you taking advantage of it? Are you receiving the blessings that are in front of you? One of my greatest strengths is in taking risks. Every opportunity you take means embracing risk and living in the unknown. The better you learn how to live the unknown, the more you evolve.

Thank you from the depths of our souls for inviting us into your world. It is an honor. We have the confidence that we are going to get to know each other throughout this process. As avid book readers, we know how intimate the relationship is between author and reader. It isn't a one-way conversation. When you participate in the exercises and apply the protocols recommended in these chapters, we can feel you shifting! Many blessings, support, love and healing from us to you.

Desiree and Alonto

[CHAPTER 2]

You are a Magnet

Every moment of existence, *you are a magnet.*

Your external world mirrors your internal world, the evidence of which is all around you. There is no break from creating our life. Every thought and emotion, conscious or unconscious, is a ripple you put out into this divine matrix. The question to ask ourselves is:

What am I a magnet of?

Your thoughts influence the flavor of emotions you experience. Those emotions then influence your heart's magnetic field. Every emotion you experience has its own signature frequency that emanates out into the field, therefore,

your emotions are your magnets.

Sometimes we think our feelings are our own and no one else understands us. In reality, people around you do pick up on your emotions. Nothing is hidden in your mind

11

or stays just to yourself. This is why I personally take my emotional/spiritual wellbeing as a serious responsibility. Not just for my sake, but also for the wellbeing of the people around me. My health affects the health of the 7.7 billion people on this planet, just as yours does. You matter greatly, my friend. So much more than you give yourself credit for. You are the beginning of a ripple that reaches across the span of this planet and beyond.

To understand this concept, we must dive into one of the most important laws of the Universe: *The Law of Resonance.*

The Law of Resonance determines precisely *what* is attracted to you based on the frequency of energy that you project from your thoughts, beliefs and emotions. The projected energy can only harmonize with energies that vibrate or resonate at a similar harmonious frequency, which then determines and creates your physical results.

Here is an illustration of how the Law of Resonance works. A tuning fork is a two-pronged steel device which is able to vibrate and emit a frequency when it is struck. It is surrounded by "the field". The field is used to describe all that exists in the Universe. It contains infinite possibilities and allows information in the form of frequencies to travel easily. A frequency has the ability to contain specific information, such as sound, thoughts, feelings, etc. When two tuning forks are placed in proximity with one another, each has the ability to affect the other. The illustration on the next page gives a great visual of this.

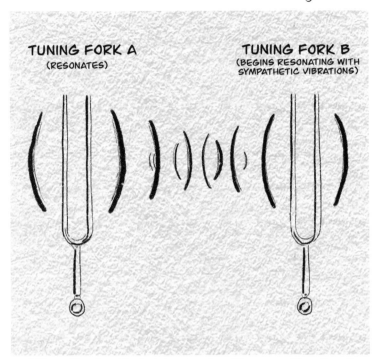

TUNING FORK A
(RESONATES)

TUNING FORK B
(BEGINS RESONATING WITH
SYMPATHETIC VIBRATIONS)

When Tuning Fork A is struck with a specific vibration, the frequency travels through the field to Tuning Fork B. Tuning Fork B then receives the information and begins to resonate with the vibrational pattern of Tuning Fork A. The frequencies match and even when Tuning Fork A is muted, Tuning Fork B will continue to emit the original frequency until a new one is introduced.

This has a strong correlation between you and Universal Energy. The Universal Energy Field seeks to match your frequency. For example, if you were to emit a frequency of distrust out into the field, you then draw distrusting relationships from the field. The field does not judge or play favorites, even though it may seem like it at times. It only harmonizes to the "tune" of your being-ness. The field can only resonate to the frequencies you are putting out.

Imagine, you turn on the radio because you want to listen to your favorite country-music station. You tune into *Classic Country 98.1* and expect to hear a song like, "Friends in Low Places" by Garth Brooks, but instead, a hardcore techno song starts playing. Would that ever happen?! Most certainly not. When you dial into a country music station you will hear country music. When you dial into a techno music station, you will hear techno music. What you hear, see, and experience is based on the frequency channel that you have chosen to tune into.

Most people have wants and desires that are different than what they are "tuned into". What station are you currently playing? It is valuable work to bring awareness to the frequencies you maintain and to change the ones that suck. The people and circumstances around you will shift when you shift. How wonderful is it that we have the power to change anything that is not working for us? We simply have to change the station!

It is also appropriate at this time to touch on another Universal Law known as the *Law of Attraction*. This Law became popular in the last couple of decades. The Law of Attraction states that the thoughts we hold eventually materialize into physical reality. In basic terms, all thoughts turn into things. Here is the caveat: the thoughts can only turn into things if the emotion associated with that thought is persistent and intense. Remember those requirements: **persistent** and **intense.**

Not every thought randomly materializes. If you think about a deer, it doesn't show up immediately in your living room. However, if you regularly think of a deer with great fondness and love for them, the Law of Attraction and the Law of Resonance work to bring a deer across your path. The Law of Attraction and the Law of Resonance truly complement one another, and they cannot exist without each other. They are the Yin and Yang of manifestation.

Next time you are experiencing a particular emotion, pay attention to its intensity levels. The stronger the emotion, the more likely it is that you will continue to attract it. Remember, your *feelings* are your magnets. There are small magnets with a weak force for attraction and large magnets with a greater force for attraction. The stronger the emotion, the bigger the magnet. Work to intensify the feelings surrounding what you desire to manifest instead of intensifying that which you don't want.

Because you are a part of the Universal Energy Field, you are connected to *all that is.* We all carry within us all of the frequencies that exist in the Universe, just like we all contain the same basic DNA. Yet we are not all the same. It is the expression of the DNA that makes us unique, and it is the expression of the frequencies that determine what we attract.

All of us are affecting one another all of the time. We are all Tuning Fork A in the example given earlier, broadcasting our energies into the field, and having those energies reflected back to us, as evidenced by our external results. But we are all also Tuning Fork B. There are certain people and places that deeply influence and draw out different frequencies from us than our regularly scheduled programming. When a person that we are near, or an environment that we are in, has energies that are clear, focused and intense, those energies can be awakened within us. Have you ever heard of the saying, *"you become the average of the five people you hang around with"*? Take inventory of those five important people in how they live, what they say, what they do, how they feel, their life circumstances, etc. Do you see similarities in their reality to yours?

You affect others and others affect you. The important thing is to be aware and deliberate with your own vibrations, and the vibrations in which you expose yourself to. This is a participatory universe. You are a participant and you continually affect the direction in which this world and human consciousness evolves.

In this book, we will work both at the level of thoughts and the level of emotions to create real transformation. Changing the mindset is not enough, as it would result in fleeting outcomes. If you are familiar with my work in "I am Fabulous" and "I am Worthy", you understand that I don't do superficial work. We dig into the wounds, love on them, thank them, and become anew. My goal is to connect you with your higher Self, channel inspiration and energetic flow, and express the music of your soul.

Money Magnet

In holistic medicine, it is understood that there is no separation between the physical and the non-physical. Whatever you do to the body, you do to the spirit. And whatever you do to the spirit, you do to the body. This is how money works as well. Our relationship with money reflects the flow of energy in our body and spirit. How you do one thing is how you do everything.

Money = Energy

Money is a symbol of energy flow. Another name for money is *currency*. The word currency has a Latin root *currens*, which means "in circulation". The very definition of money already highlights the importance of *flow*. Money is a medium of energy exchange. You must create flow within you for money to flow towards you. *Chronic* anger, hopelessness, fear, worry, grief and shame constrict energy flow and block your ability to receive money. Please note the emphasis placed on the word *chronic*. As human beings, we are designed to experience all emotions. Feeling anger is not the problem. The problem lies in the disease that takes root after 15 years of experiencing that same anger and holding onto it within the body. The next chapters will dive into the releasing of those trapped emotions that are affecting not only our physical health, but also the health of our finances.

All of us, in this current moment, are inhaling oxygen without even thinking about it. There is plenty all around us and we never have to worry about having enough air to breathe. When we inhale, do we need to worry about taking too much of it from the person sitting next to us? That's absurd! There is enough oxygen in the atmosphere for 7.7

billion people on this planet. As we emphasized earlier, Zig Ziglar said, "money is like oxygen". That would mean that money is ever-abundant just like the air that is available to us.

The only thing that would keep us from the amount of air we can breathe in, is how deep we are inhaling and exhaling. When anxiety strikes, breath is shallow. The amount of oxygen that is able to be received is limited. But when the anxious frequency is cleared, relaxation occurs and deeper breaths resume. As a result, more energy flows throughout the entire body.

As we work on releasing chronic, low-frequency emotions that create stagnation, our capacity to receive more, expands. Once we receive, the energy doesn't stop there. After that deep inhale which nourishes our bodies, a large exhale follows. In creating a release for us, we are releasing carbon dioxide. It is the very substance that the plants around us need to be able to sustain their life and continue to create oxygen. The more you receive, the more you can give. And the more you give, the more you are able to receive. That principle rings true for everything! When you receive more love, don't you have a desire to share that loving energy with others?

When that life-giving flow of receiving and giving is stopped, death is inevitable. You can't hold your breath and expect to live. The same is true for money. Just like air, money is ever present in the world. And it *needs* to circulate, as the word *currency* denotes. It isn't designed to be stagnant. Money will flow in the world no matter what. Wouldn't it be great to have money flow into the hands of more people than just a few? Life is not a zero-sum game in an Infinite Universe. There is *so* much more available to you, my friend. You can create flow and become a money magnet!

The Method

As a practitioner of Chinese Medicine, our entire job description is to create and maintain the proper flow of energy in all of the organs and meridians in the body. The basic principle is this:

When there is free flow,

there is no pain.

When there is no free flow,

there is pain.

Stagnation of energy is the beginning of disease. Before physical stagnation manifests (i.e. inflammation, pain, atherosclerosis, tumors, cysts, etc.), it first begins with energetic stagnation. This is why acupuncture is the best form of preventative medicine. Acupuncturists see the energetic stagnation before it becomes dense matter and transforms into physical disease.

We can feel, hear, smell and see the subtle stagnations at their beginning stages by feeling the pulse, observing the tongue and the body, palpating channels and points, hearing the voice, asking questions and connecting with your energy pattern. Some practitioners have such extreme sensitivities that they can tell if a woman is pregnant simply by the feel of her pulse. It may sound mysterious to many, but it takes a lifetime of practice to master these specific skills of observation.

Every feeling has its own vibratory pattern, which in turn will influence the energy flow of specific organs and chakras. Certain frequencies will create expansion and flow, while others create contraction and stagnation. Within this book, we will work on the chronic, persistent and intense vibrations that are creating stagnation.

Here is a three-step process that is the undertone of the work. Chinese Medicine is extraordinary at following a sequence to arrive at the desired flow of energy.

1. **Clear the Obstruction** We must bring awareness to the obstructive frequency and then take steps to remove it. When a person holds onto the frequency of *distrust,* for example, then the first step would be to release that frequency out of their system.

2. **Nourish** After the obstruction is removed, a new pattern of frequency must be introduced to replace that which has been cleared. Clearing is not enough. If you don't introduce something different to replace the vacuum that is left behind, it is possible for one to regress and return to the old pattern. In this scenario, the frequency of *trust* would be introduced, so that the person can familiarize themselves within this new feeling.

3. **Harmonize** This is the final step that creates the lasting change. Harmonization is taking the new frequency and deeply integrating it into the system. This step acts like

the glue that makes the new frequency stick, so that *trust* becomes the person's new normal. The spirit is less likely to reject the new frequency when it has been harmonized.

The feeling you no longer want that is causing destruction, chaos and disharmony in your life is the obstruction that we are working to **clear**. Creating a new paradigm, or a new perspective, is the process of **nourishing**. Emotional impact and intensity through the use of essential oils is how we **harmonize** this new you.

You will know that the above method has become a success when this aspect of yourself, such as trusting, has become an automatic habit and you participate in it without conscious effort or strain.

When we harmonize with essential oils, we are incorporating all three of these elements in one. This approach makes it easy to break through the natural body/spirit resistance to change and the body willingly incorporates your new habits.

There are many techniques to break free from the limited self. A few of my favorites have included yoga, tai chi, qi gong, tapping, acupuncture, chiropractic care, meditation, general exercise, juicing, saunas, cleanses, prayer and much more! In the last several years, I have also added essential oils to my toolbox, and it has made a world of difference.

Alonto and I have since become avid essential oil users. Because of my background, I have been able to combine essential oils and known Chinese Medical principles to create a unique process that shifts energy flow in a quick and effective manner that we will be using throughout our time together.

If you already have essential oils for this process, please make sure they are pure and therapeutic-grade. The quality of the oils significantly impacts the ability to move energetic stagnations. The kind you purchase at most health food stores are subpar. The ones found at a gas station or big box retailers are even worse. When it comes to the high-quality work we are about to embark on within this book, you will want access to the highest quality essential oils to match. If you do not have essential oils yet, or would like to upgrade your current collection, please contact me through my website: www.desireemangandog.com

tial Oil List

- [ ] LIME
- [ ] MAGNOLIA
- [ ] MARJORAM
- [ ] PATCHOULI
- [ ] PEPPERMINT
- [ ] PINK PEPPER
- [ ] ROMAN CHAMOMILE
- [ ] ROSE
- [ ] SIBERIAN FIR
- [ ] SPIKENARD
- [ ] TEA TREE
- [ ] TUMERIC
- [ ] WILD ORANGE
- [ ] WINTERGREEN
- [ ] YLANG YLANG

- [ ] FRANKINCENSE
- [ ] GREEN MANDARIN
- [ ] HELICHRYSUM
- [ ] INDIAN SANDALWOOD
- [ ] LAVENDER
- [ ] LEMONGRASS

OPTIONAL OILS FOR DIFFUSER BLENDS:
- [ ] GINGER
- [ ] JUNIPER BERRY
- [ ] LEMON

[CHAPTER 3]

The Magnetic Framework

It had been two days. Two whole days of watching in frustration as my husband obsessed over our son's *Rubik's Cube.* How he was dedicating that much time and energy into that small, square toy was beyond me. I simply do not have that kind of patience. But if there is anything I know about Alonto, it's that when he has decided on something, he is going to make it happen. I can appreciate that. I understand the need to solve problems and feel accomplished. And much to my surprise, this particular problem ended up also providing us with a very valuable lesson.

I've always been obsessed with playing games. I love the satisfaction that comes with solving puzzles and finding solutions. It's a passion that has been with me for as long as I can remember. Even when I was just six years old, my mother bought me a Rubik's Cube. I was so determined to solve it! But it didn't take long for me to get very frustrated with it. Every time I would attempt to conquer it, I would get part way through and give up. It was impossible! I felt it was up there with magic: way out of my realm of comprehension. You could say that I have been frustrated with that toy my whole life. 😔

Then, a couple of days ago, I saw my son's cube out of the corner of my eye. My great nemesis had returned! Curiosity got the best of me. Did I have what it takes to solve that thing once and for all? I decided to give it another shot. This time, I was approaching it with a little help from one of my all-time favorite resources: YouTube!

There are phenomenal instructors within reach on YouTube. I did a quick search on "solving a Rubik's Cube" and realized it *was* possible! One YouTuber outlined a process and framework that provided a way for *anyone* to solve it. After ten hours of diligently working the process and implementing the very strategies that he taught, I solved the Rubik's Cube for the first time! It was a cause for major celebration! The family cheered, hollered, and jumped up and down. I think Desiree was the one that was the most excited, though. She wanted to get back to writing this book! 😄

It took me 33 years to finally accomplish my childhood goal. And without the guidance that I found by watching YouTube, there's no doubt in my mind that I still wouldn't have finished it. I needed to identify the systems and frameworks in order to unlock that seemingly impossible puzzle. It helped me to understand that anything can be demystified by being guided through the inner-workings and strategies that experts utilize. Maybe for you, this is how money and success feel: like a magical puzzle that you don't understand.

While I was wrapped up in trying to solve the Rubik's Cube, there was a moment before the final step where I thought I had messed up again. I was so close to being consumed by frustration, but instead, I reminded myself to trust the steps that the instructor had given. Moments later, it was complete! I believe persistence is truly the mother of all skills. Because with persistence and a trusted guide, nothing is out of reach! With those two things, you can become skilled at attracting huge amounts of money just like I was able to become skilled at solving the impossible Rubik's Cube.

Alonto and I are honored that you have trusted *us* to be your guides. Many of the people we work with tell us that they don't understand how money works. Maybe you fall within this same category. We understand and want you to know: you're not alone. Majority of the belief systems that our society currently carries about money are truly dysfunctional and it can be a challenge to not have adopted some of it into your psyche. But you picked up this book for a reason! It is my belief that you will always find what you are seeking. If something is important enough to you, the best mentors will always come along your path to help you figure it out. We are honored to help you rewrite your current money story into something much more beautiful using the *"I am Magnetic"* Framework.

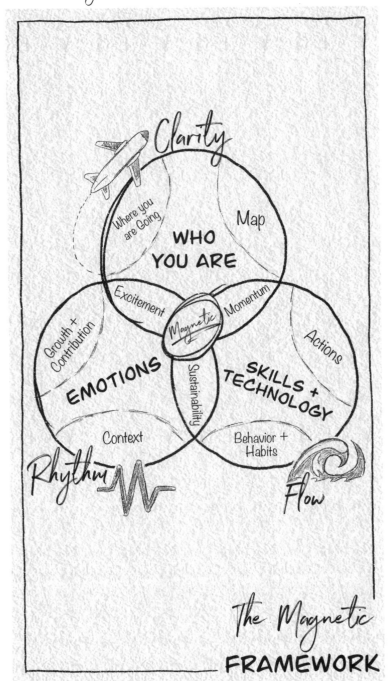

This diagram outlines the three components for creating and attracting your desired outcomes, especially in relation to the flow of money. Implementing these techniques will change your worn money narrative to reflect more expansiveness.

All that you need to accomplish this is *Clarity, Flow* and *Rhythm.* When each of these is in order, a magnetic zone is unlocked where synchronicities abound, and creation feels effortless. The "treading through mud" experience that we have all felt before becomes a distant memory. 😍

We have all been blessed with seasons of flow, whether it was consciously or unconsciously created. Jamie Wheal and Steven Kotler brilliantly outlined this "flow state" in their book *Stealing Fire*. They created the acronym *STER*.

Selflessness: The ego dies and a feeling of being connected to all of humanity and the Universe is created

Timelessness: A sense of time disappears and there is extreme presence (i.e. three hours can feel like one minute)

Effortlessness: Things happen without force

Richness of Information: A download of information that is crystal clear

STER helps to identify everything that needs to align in order for the "flow state" to be activated. As we have mentioned before, this "flow state" is where the art of being magnetic lies. It is the destination. The breakdown of the three components in the *"I am Magnetic" Framework* can help you to understand what specifically needs to come together in order for you to get there.

Note: there is no need to answer the following questions in this chapter. It is a prelude to the next chapters where the writing begins.

Clarity

Clarity is the state of being easily visible, understood, heard and free from ambiguity.

First, it is important to have clarity in *who you are.*

What is important to you? What do you value the most?

Developing clarity on who you are at your core helps you to develop an inner-compass that can guide your every decision. Life is a jungle, with many distractions designed to take you off course. A compass is necessary to guide you. It can help keep you from frustration and wandering mindlessly about.

Second, have clarity on *what you want to be known for.*

What contributions do you want to make in society? What journey and destination do you desire to experience?

This is essentially your map, outlining point A to point B and highlighting the different stops along the way that you would like to make. It gives your compass a purpose.

Third, have clarity on *how you are going to get there.*

What is the vehicle you are utilizing to foster the things that are important to you? What methodology fits your values?

There are many different companies, organizations and disciplines you can get into. Choosing the vehicle that matches your values will make the journey fun, exciting and sustainable.

Flow

Flow is the action of moving along in a steady, continuous stream.

Flow = Life

Notice, this is different than the "flow state" that was mentioned earlier. The "flow state" is the destination. It is what is created as these components are activated within you. Flow is one of these necessary components. It refers to the workings of the inner body and spirit.

Fluidity of thoughts and emotions is the foundation for growth and expansion. We cannot experience the same energetic patterns over and over and expect a different outcome. Let go of the past. Break free from the old programs that have been repeating for years. When you have the same, old story, you will suffer from the same, old problems. If you find yourself complaining about the same thing over and over again, you can *guarantee* there is no flow.

First, identify the current money story you hold in your subconscious and chip away at those paradigms. This includes the thought patterns as well as the painful emotions associated with your money story. *Clear* the stagnations of old and destructive money beliefs.

Second, introduce a new money story with elevated emotions to instill expansive frequency patterns. This produces the focus and intensity that are needed for graceful manifestation. The new, empowering thoughts and feelings are what we *nourish* to upgrade our reality.

Third, train your spirit to experience life from the perspective of abundance and wholeness. *Harmonize* by making the new pattern a habit. When you embody this new way of "being" and automatically get there without great effort, you will have proof that the new pattern has successfully harmonized.

Rhythm

Rhythm is a strong, regular, repeated pattern of movement or sound.

It is necessary to hear and feel the pulse of the Earth and to adjust to the changing seasons she provides. Even the sun rising in the morning and setting again in the evening demonstrates her purposeful balance. Nature is filled with cycles of Yin and Yang. Yin provides the times of rest, nourishment and descending of energy. Yang provides the times of activity, expansion and the rising of energy. Yin and Yang are opposites, yet complementary. Together they complete the picture of wholeness.

Yin and Yang are opposites, yet complementary.

What is the rhythm of your soul? Are you in sync with yourself? Are you aligned with nature and your physical environment?

When a dancer demonstrates the rhythm perfectly on time with their movements, it is exhilerating to watch. You know it's magical when your chest tingles with excitement and the hairs on your arms rise. But when a dancer is off, even by a little, it causes you to cringe.

The question I challenge you to ask yourself is this: do you make others' chests tingle with excitement or do you make them cringe? Are people inspired when they observe your life or do they feel the need to look away? We must take accountability for the cringe-worthy aspects of our lives and be willing to change where it is necessary.

First, we will learn how to be on beat with the cycles of yin and yang. It's important to tune into your personal rhythm and the rhythm of the *whole* collective.

Second, we will evaluate and adjust environmenal influences that are affecting your soul's rhythm.

Third, we will learn the art of giving and receiving. Most of us are phenomenal givers, yet poor receivers. Both activities must happen in order to become a money magnet.

Before we begin:

Thank yourself for taking the time in your life to change how you think and feel about money. Most people hold the same money narrative for their entire life and rob themselves of unique and magical experiences. Many don't think money is important to master, nor do they realize the connection between emotional and financial maturity. Breaking through money limitations can help you to discover the depths of your beautiful spirit.

The following chapters include tools and techniques that create energetic shifts within you. As you move through the exercises and applications, note that a variety of symptoms can occur when breaking through stagnant energy. If you experience any of the following, look at it as a *healing crisis.* It is nothing to be alarmed about. These symptoms could happen for a couple of minutes or last up to 24 hours.

Please honor your process of releasing and trust that the emotional healing is taking place. On the other hand, if you don't experience any of these symptoms, it doesn't mean that the process isn't working. It only showcases the fact that we all move through things in our own unique ways.

Here are some possible side effects:
-dizziness
-fatigue
-a feeling of heaviness in the body
-headache
-nausea
-an out-of-body experience

-heat flushes
-a desire for solitude
-body aches
-moodiness
-irritability/anger
-sadness
-a brief wave of anxiousness
-increased urination and/or bowel movements
-returning to old addictions for a day
-cold/flu
-migratory body pain
-energy surges
-temporary change in sleep pattern

You may proceed through this material as quickly or as slowly as you wish. I only ask that you follow the chapters sequentially. You may desire to take an entire day to work through it, or perhaps you want to spread it out over two weeks. For the greatest results, I wouldn't recommend taking longer than one month to complete the material.

This process can then be repeated over and over again. Whenever you feel stagnant in your creativity, workflow, finances, relationships, and life in general, the *"I am Magnetic"* process has the ability to course-correct the direction you are heading.

Results and Expectations:

You should expect *progress*. For some, this means experiencing a huge surge in gains, and for others it will be more incremental. There will also be seasons where one will experience incremental growth for a while, and then a huge surge will take place, or vice versa. As long as there is some kind of progress, that is all that matters.

The best way to measure progress is by documenting your journey. First, have a journal to record your thoughts, emotions, and the happenings of your life. Second, take the time to record every penny that comes in at the end of the day. You may choose to use a spreadsheet, a piece of paper, or an app. Either way, you will want to include paychecks, PayPal payments, gift cards, tangible money, etc.

Denise Duffield Thomas helped me to understand that this isn't an accounting exercise. There is no need to feel overwhelmed about it. Instead, it's an exercise to become aware of how much you actually bring in. You won't know if progress is being made if you don't take the time to record numbers throughout the process. At a minimum, take the time to record your income at the end of each week. If you only do it once a month, you will be less connected to your wealth-creation process.

My dear soul-friend,

Let's become

Magnetic!

(To what you really want...)

[CHAPTER 4]

The Road is Clear

The windows were rolled down and my arm hung outside of the car as I cruised happily down I-5 towards San Diego. I was in a great mood having just visited a friend in Santa Monica. I could smell the fresh ocean breeze and smiled as "California Love" came through my CD player. It was a picture-perfect day.

Suddenly, I felt a chill as I passed through Carlsbad. I looked down and realized that there was moisture on my hand. I pulled my arm inside the car, and as I surveyed the road ahead, I noticed a faint amount of fog and blinking yellow hazard lights. I took my foot off the gas pedal and slowed down, concerned about what may lie ahead.

As I continued on, the fog became so thick that all I could see was pure white all around me. I was instantly filled with anxiety. I couldn't see in front of me! I was sure others wouldn't be able to see me, either.

I slowed down to a mere 10mph. I crawled at this pace, hyper-focused on all that could go wrong, for the next three miles. Finally, the fog began to lift. The road slowly became clearer and clearer and all of us began to return to the "California Speed Limit" (at least 10mph over what is posted).

The fog had slowed my momentum! I continued on my journey, reflecting on how dramatic the shift was from clear roads to fog and back to clear again. I couldn't help but draw a metaphor from that situation to every other time in my life when I found myself significantly slowed down in my progress, as if a metaphorical fog was creating a blurry, indistinct path. It wasn't until the fog lifted that things could progress again. Sometimes the fog would clear up quickly, but I could think of many times when it would linger and create drastic delays in my accomplishments. I'm sure you can relate! How many goals have been delayed or given up on altogether because of this "foggy feeling"?

"When the road is unclear, you take hesitant steps."

—Alonto Mangandog

Clarity is what gives us the confidence to move forward with intensity. It is what allows limits to be stretched to see what you are actually capable of. While I was driving, it took the fog physically lifting for the road to become clear. I was then able to confidently and quickly proceed forward on the highway towards my destination.

When we don't know what's in front of us, uneasiness is created. Some of the anxiety we experience is simply due to lack of clarity. But clarity can be figured out! And once it is experienced, peace will be felt about the path you find yourself on.

One of my greatest pet peeves when consulting a client is when they say, "I don't know" as an answer to why they are having a setback that we are trying to work through. That phrase is the ultimate form of avoidance and keeps a person in a nebulous state of existence. Progress cannot happen with an *"I don't know".* Majority of the time, the answer is known. But the truth is being avoided because we either don't want to admit the shame we feel, or perhaps we think our dream is too outrageously big and impossible to create, so we refuse to speak of it at all.

I end up challenging those I consult with to dig deeper and to be honest with what *is* known. "Knowing" often means that we are facing our pain, our shame, and our setbacks. That can be extremely uncomfortable for some because as Anthony Robbins teaches, the desire to avoid pain is one of our main motivators. It even outweighs the desire to seek pleasure.

There are many methods to help fight the discomfort and uncover the truth. I have found *using essential oils* to be one of them. I also have found that sharing these honest thoughts and feelings with a loving friend or partner is helpful. It is therapeutic and healing to give voice to our pains and fears, especially if it has never been spoken of before.

Some people avoid discussing their thoughts with others for fear of being seen as a *complainer*. But it is important to note that there is a difference between complaining and acknowledging. Acknowledging is a way to release trapped energy and feel liberated from its shackles. How sweet it is for two friends or partners to create a safe space between them of non-judgment, listening in love and being vulnerable with one another.

Writing in a journal is another great option, for it is an additional form of speaking. There will be many opportunities to write here in this book, as it's one of my favorite tools for the healing process.

When Alonto shared his story of driving through a fog, I could feel how unnerved he was. Thankfully, he had a "compass" or a guiding force, in the form of his GPS to guide him through the times when he literally couldn't see in front of him. Our objective is to identify your compass so you will have it to direct you through your fog. If you remember, energy flows where attention goes. Staying in the fog, being uncertain and lacking clarity about your next steps, constricts your energy. A compass is necessary to create a clear direction in order for your energy to flow freely.

The *"Don't Want"* Dump or DWD

Before we clarify your direction and discover your personal compass, we must first purge all of the things you do not want out of your personal energy field. These are creating the fog that is all around you, covering your path and slowing down your progress. Within these next pages, you have complete permission to have a "bitch-fest"! This is a safe space for you to complain, criticize, grumble and whine because it is for a *constructive* purpose. We will be using all of the negativity that comes out of this clearing exercise to provide clarity and make it easier to identify what you *do* want.

Give yourself the space and freedom to write *anything* you don't like. To ensure you are including everything in your life that is unsatisfying, let's diffuse some beneficial essential oils.

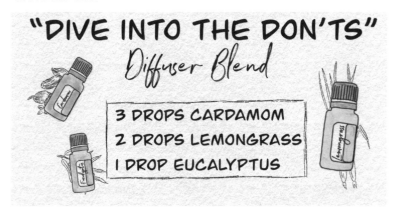

"DIVE INTO THE DON'TS"
Diffuser Blend

3 DROPS CARDAMOM
2 DROPS LEMONGRASS
1 DROP EUCALYPTUS

"Dive into the Don'ts" diffuser blend helps bring awareness to what needs attention. Think of your complaints like a "check-engine light". It's a warning sign that something is

out of alignment internally. These are gifts that are attempting to bring you back into alignment.

Cardamom works well to bring conscious awareness to the subconscious patterns. It also helps digest difficult emotions. Cardamom is the essential oil of choice when it's time to dig deep and deal with painful, uncomfortable feelings. The goal is to get you to feel the anguish of your "don't wants", so that the pain propels you towards your dreams and desires. Cardamom is also excellent in relieving irritability from the disgruntled soul.

Lemongrass follows cardamom. As cardamom helps you to see and feel the pain, lemongrass comes in to clear out the stagnation. As you write out your complaints, lemongrass will loosen the grip of pessimism and misery that is often entangled in the lungs.

Eucalyptus is our nourishing and harmonizing essential oil within this blend. Its main function is to circulate and transport out what lemongrass has liberated. Eucalyptus provides comfort and allows you to breathe easier, as if a friend has their hand on your shoulder, reminding you that "everything is going to be okay".

Now is the time!

Get that diffuser blend going and write the things that make you unhappy in the following pages. The *Wheel of Life* can help! Even though this is a money book, all of these areas affect overall energy flow. Future chapters will dive specifically into limiting money beliefs, so don't feel like you have to write all of your money blocks in this chapter.

I DON'T WANT...

I am unhappy with... **I hate...**

I'm dissatisfied with...

I'm mad about...

I'm sick of... I'm worried that...

I'M SCARED OF...

I'm tired of... I can't stand...

_____

_____

_____

_____

_____

_____

_____

_____

_____

_____

_____

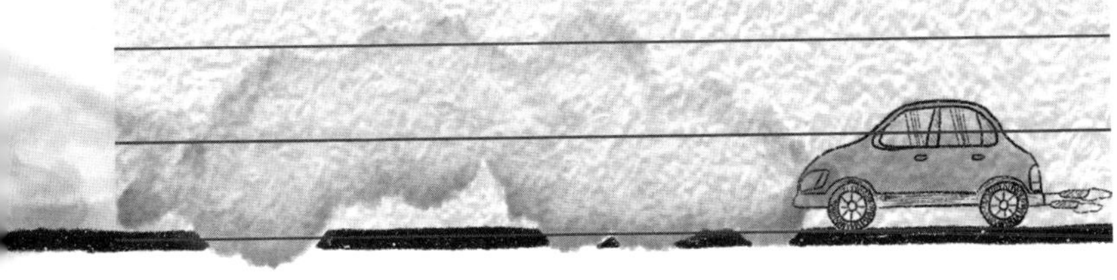

Once you have finished writing out your "I don't want"s...

APPLY *Tea Tree* TO YOUR CHEST AND HEART SPACE. INHALE THE REST OF THE AROMA FROM YOUR HANDS.

APPLY *Frankincense* (ONE DROP) TO THE BOTTOM OF EACH FOOT.

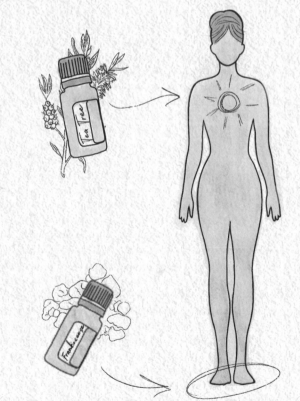

Tea Tree: This essential oil cleanses any residue that is left behind even after lemongrass has been diffused. It will feel like a reset.

Frankincense: This oil nourishes all of the areas where stagnant energy has been released out of your system. It also stirs all of the things that you do not want within your soul and also reveals all that is right for you.

Who are you?

It's a complex question for such a layered and intricate being! And while we can't promise you the answer in its entirety, perhaps it would be beneficial to you to have a tool that will align you more with your truth.

Every day is filled with numerous evaluations and decisions. We are constantly asked to decide what is best for us, what we should be focusing on, what priorities need attention, etc. If you lack clarity in who you are and what you value, it is nearly impossible to make the great daily decisions that lead you towards the extraordinary outcomes.

"You cannot make it as a wandering generality, you must become a meaningful specific." -Zig Ziglar

Imagine with me that you are in the middle of a jungle. When you look north, you see trees. When you look south, you see trees. East and west also provide the same view. Lacking a compass to guide you to your destination point, the probability of arriving there is slim to none. With a compass and a specific destination, you have a much better chance. You can develop momentum knowing that whenever you need to, you can check-in with your compass to verify if the direction you're heading in is accurate.

Personally, I have a horrible sense of direction, especially when it comes to driving in my city. I am eternally grateful for Google Maps! Before I take off from home, I put the address into my app and the best path appears. Even when I take a wrong turn, Google Maps (my compass) adjusts and reroutes me to get back on track to my destination. No matter what "mistakes" I make, an opportunity to realign always presents itself.

By accomplishing this next exercise, *The Values Compass*, you will be equipped with a tool that can do the same for you. It won't matter what mistakes you make, what detours you choose to take, or how similarly confusing the scenery around you gets, your personal compass will be there to guide you, reroute you, and get you back on course. In order to make this an easier process, we will begin by first utilizing an essential oil application protocol. These essential oils will promote self-realization and make your decisions obvious rather than have you spiral into an identity crisis.

Fennel has a way of cutting through the "excess"

Self-Realization Protocol

APPLY *Fennel* TO THE OUTSIDE OF BOTH OF THE WRIST CREASES

APPLY *Lavender* ON THE REN 17 ACUPUNCTURE POINT

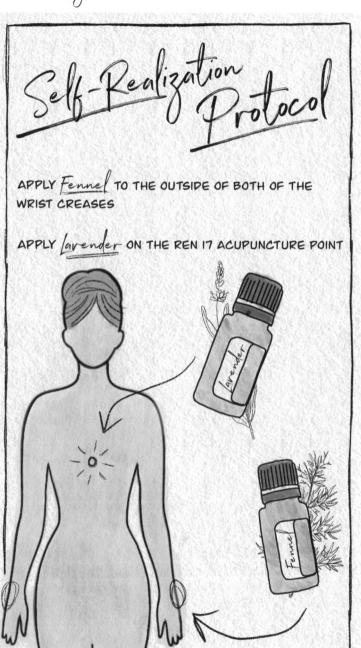

information that is not in alignment. Throughout our lives, people have provided input that may or may not be accurate. Parents, teachers, friends, partners, bosses, co-workers and more have all given feedback that may not be true, yet we have adopted it as being so. Fennel sifts through the untrue beliefs we have identified with, leaving us with a more accurate representation of our core values. Whenever realignment is needed, Fennel comes to the rescue. Please note, if you deal with sensitive skin, ensure that you dilute the Fennel with Fractionated Coconut Oil before or after application.

The San Jiao meridian passes through the outside of the wrist crease. It is an "invisible organ" that translates to "triple heater". The role of San Jiao is water metabolism and temperature regulation. Because it regulates how our body adjusts to the external environment, I apply essential oils to this meridian when adjusting to the energies of other people.

Lavender is an oil that improves communication not only with others, but also with ourselves. Since we cleared away much of our external noise in the *"Don't Want Dump"* section, Lavender will turn up the volume of your inner voice. It acts as a pure, innocent, beautifully divine voice that gently nudges you to speak up. Lavender reveals your unique *Values Compass* without the influence of others' opinions. After all, this should be a conversation between you and the Divine.

Ren 17 is between the breasts or nipple line. It is "Shan Zhong", or chest center. Lavender applied to Ren 17 unbinds the chest and creates better access to your core essence.

Values Compass

Directions

1. Take a look at the following lists and put a circle around each of the values that resonate with you. Don't be limited by a number. We will narrow them down as we progress through the exercise.

I value...

ADVENTURE!
>> RISK ✓
>> THE UNKNOWN ✓
>> THRILL
>> DANGER
>> SPECULATION
>> GAMBLING
>> ENDEAVORS
>> QUESTS
>> EXPERIMENTATION
>> EXHILERATION ✓

CONTRIBUTING!
>> SERVICE
>> IMPROVEMENT ✓
>> AUGMENTATION
>> ASSISTANCE
>> STRENGTHENING ✓
>> FACILITATION
>> MINISTERING
>> PROVIDING

DISCOVERING!
>> LEARNING ✓
>> DETECTION
>> PERCEIVING
>> LOCATING
>> REALIZATION ✓
>> UNCOVERING ✓
>> DISCERNMENT ✓
>> DISTINGUISHMENT
>> OBSERVATION

CREATING!
>> DESIGN
>> INVENTION
>> PERFECTING
>> IMAGINATION ✓
>> INGENUITY
>> ORIGINALITY ✓
>> ASSEMBLY
>> PLANNING
>> BUILDING

I value...

RELATING!
>> CONNECTION ✓
>> FAMILY
>> COMMUNITY
>> UNITY
>> NURTURING
>> BONDING
>> INTEGRATION
>> BEING WITH

FEELING!
>> EMOTIONS ✓
>> SENSATIONS ✓
>> ALIGNMENT ✓
>> GOOD VIBRATIONS ✓
>> ENERGY ✓
>> FLOW ✓
>> FEELING GOOD ✓

CATALYZING!
>> IMPACTING
>> ENCOURAGMENT
>> ENERGIZING ✓
>> ALTERING
>> REPAIRING
>> ACTIVATION ✓
>> COACHING ✓
>> SPARKING
>> MOVING FORWARD ✓

SPIRITUALITY!
>> AWARENESS ✓
>> ACCEPTANCE ✓
>> BEING "AWAKE" ✓
>> DEVOTION
>> HOLINESS
>> HONOR
>> PASSION ✓
>> RELIGION

BEAUTY!
>> GRACE
>> ELEGANCE
>> ATTRACTIVENESS
>> RADIANCE ✓

MASTERY!
>> EXPERTISE
>> DOMINATION
>> SUPERIORITY
>> EXCELLENCE ✓
>> BEING THE BEST

PLEASURE!
>> HAVING FUN ✓
>> SENSUALITY
>> PHYSICALITY
>> BLISS ✓
>> AMUSEMENT

I value...

WINNING!
>> ACCOMPLISHMENT ✓
>> SCORING
>> WINNING OVER
>> TRIUMPH
>> ACQUIRING

LEADING!
>> GUIDING
>> INSPIRATION ✓
>> INFLUENCE ✓
>> GOVERNING
>> RULING
>> PERSUASION
>> ENCOURAGEMENT ✓

TEACHING!
>> EDUCATION ✓
>> INSTRUCTION
>> ENLIGHTENMENT ✓
>> INFORMATION
>> PREPARATION
>> EXPLANATION

SENSITIVITY!
>> COMPASSION ✓
>> TENDERNESS ✓
>> TOUCH ✓
>> PERCEPTION ✓
>> PRESENCE ✓
>> EMPATHY ✓

"...your values become your destiny."
—Ghandi

2. Write down the **TOP TEN** words/phrases that you have chosen in the spaces provided below.

1. _____

2. _____

3. _____

4. _____

5. _____

6. _____

7. _____

8. _____

9. _____

10. _____

3. Narrow down the list by putting a check mark next to **FIVE** of the most important values on the list above.

4. Narrow down the list even further by circling the **TOP THREE** most important values to you.

5. Finally, on the next page, write your top three values in **BIG** and **BOLD** letters.

My Top Three Values:

1.

2.

3.

Congratulations!

You have identified your *Values Compass!* In order for this exercise to be useful, you must use these values like a compass to direct you. Every decision you make must be weighed against and in alignment with your **three core values**. If not, you will get lost and distracted in the jungle of life.

Most successful people speak of having a "why" or a purpose identified that provides them with the fuel and desire to keep going and crush their goals even after the adrenaline wears off. They encourage us all to find our own, and even provide exercises to help with the identification process. But sometimes, despite our best efforts, our "why" remains unclear. Instead of feeling the nagging pressure to figure it out, use your *Values Compass!* Over time, it will become easier to identify the "why that makes you cry".

This is simple, yes. Yet, it is profound and very beneficial.

Questions

Now that you have identified your core values, it will be easier to answer the questions we contemplated earlier.

1. What is important to you? What do you value most? When you were a child, what things brought you joy?

Write all of the things in life that matter to you. What activities do you spend your time and energy on? Identify the things that cause you to lose your sense of time. What could you spend forever doing? It should be fun and joyful for you! What are you great at?

For me, I love creating recipes with essential oils that foster energetic shifts. Hence, I carry a journal around with me at all times and carve out time in my day to experiment with concoctions. I value creativity and mastery in the healing arts.

What do you value? Do you enjoy being with your family? Connecting with your community? List as many things as you can think of!

2. What do you want to be known for? What contributions would you like to make to society? How many people would you like to serve?

Be as specific as possible. Many say, "I want to help people". But that is too generic! What is the *specific* problem that you want to help people with? Who are the people that you want to help? Contemplate how many of those people you would like to personally influence. Again, be specific, not general.

3. How are you going to accomplish this? What platform would you like to utilize to share your message and gifts? What processes or systems are in alignment with your values?

"If you place the seed in the right environment, it will grow without coaxing."
-BJ Fogg

You may have the most amazing idea, or "seed". But if that seed was meant to grow in a warm climate, and instead you choose to plant it in the middle of Alaska, it won't grow. It will die. The platform is your soil and the environment that will decide how well the seed grows and if it will blossom to its fullest expression or wither away.

Maybe you love to simplify complex concepts for others. Teaching and speaking would be the platforms that grow your seed quickly. You may be an exceptional writer. In this case, writing a book, blog, or even long Instagram posts are your best platforms. Maybe you are great at listening and connecting the dots for someone else's story. Consulting or coaching may be what works best for you.

There are many platforms out there to choose from. You have to make sure you are considering which one is going to be the most efficient method for you. Write your thoughts on this specific topic on the next page.

Freedom, Creativity and Community

Your compass is comprised of your three core values. For me, this includes the freedom to live life by my design, while being creative and participating in community. Each of those values shaped my childhood and as an adult, I have found that I am happiest when I am in alignment with them. I found it helpful to create a visual representation of these things, so I had something to measure every daily decision by. My compass looks like this:

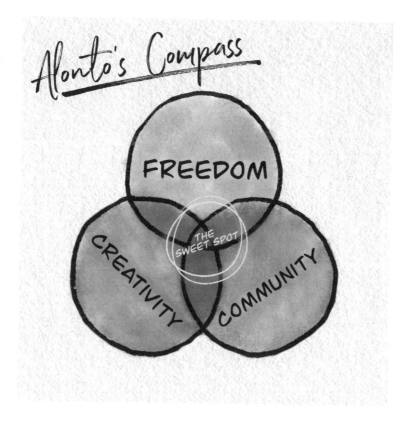

If I want to ensure that I am staying in alignment with who I really am and what I was placed on this earth to accomplish, I have to ask myself the following before making any decision:

"How does [this decision I am about to make] stay true to my compass? How does it contribute towards the impact I am designed to create?"

When my daily decisions match *each* of my three values, it is an absolute YES to proceed forward. Having answers to the questions also ensures that I know why I am saying *yes* before I even get started, which sets the entire activity out on a positive foot.

This should be an essential part of your decision-making process, too! By regularly reminding yourself of your personal truth, you can capitalize on the sweet spot of manifestation and momentum. On the next page, fill out your compass with your top three values. You can color it in, doodle on it, or add any other visual elements that will personalize it to your liking. Then, take a picture of it and keep it close to you at all times. Whenever you have a decision to make, ask yourself the same questions that I do with your personal *Values Compass* in mind.

Share your completed compass with our community! Take a picture of it and post it on the social media platform of your choosing alongside the hashtag:

#iammagneticcompass

Let others know what matters most to you and see what matters most to them!

[CHAPTER 5]

Money Makeup

What is *Money Makeup*?

Money Makeup is the composition of one's money beliefs and emotions that shape and determine their behaviors surrounding money.

Majority of your *Money Makeup* formed in your early childhood. Likely, you adopted whatever your parents, family and community taught you about money. A pastor we knew shared this analogy: "The eyes of children are like video camera lenses. They record every frame and store the information in the back of their mind. There is no discrimination or judgment in what is recorded. They just record what's there."

Our parents and respected adults have imprinted their beliefs on us, whether intentional or unintentional, constructive or destructive. We do this to our own children as well, hence the passing on of generational patterns. It can be easy to get caught in an existential crisis once you really dig into this understanding, contemplating if what you believe is who you really are or if you are just playing out what you were taught. But then you have to ask yourself, *is what I was taught who I am anyway?* And the endless loop continues...

As many of us have experienced, though, it is possible to seperate from a learned behavior. All that is needed is a willingness to learn a new paradigm. Improving your money story is certainly available to you, and it doesn't have to be as huge a feat as you may believe. In fact, it can happen faster than you think. Since you already learned one kind of money makeup as a child, we can "make up" another story that provides you with more peace, inspiration and growth.

No Shame

If you are someone who often says, *"I don't care about money,"* or *"I only want enough to meet my needs,"* I absolutely hear you. I used to say those exact same things as well. All of us have different standards and needs. What is abundance to one person may seem minimal to another. For example, when you have five children, financial demands are higher than for someone who only has one child.

The goal isn't so much to set a specific parameter for what abundance should mean to you. It is to lessen the worry and fear that you have surrounding the abundance. My goal is to move you from just *surviving* in this world to confidently thriving in it. Living in constant survival mode is quite insulting to the marvelous, magnificent, infinite being that is YOU!

Thriving is about honoring yourself and appreciating what you have to contribute to humanity. Your work is meaningful because *you* are meaningful. The opportunity to play with energy and create from the world of infinite possibilities is available to you. All you need is access to it. Liberating stagnant energies opens the doors for you. Creating flow creates access.

Whatever your desires are, you deserve it. Do you want to create a retreat center? Or a non-profit? Would you like to purchase land to build a commune? Are you interested in becoming a shaman? Do you want to create a thriving online business? Would you like to finally go on that dream trip to Maldives? Do you aspire to grow a large network marketing business? 😊

Whatever it is, I give you permission to want it and have it! Often, we are deterred in our dreams and ambitions because of the opinions of those closest to us. Due to their protection mechanism and their desire to ensure that nothing changes, they do what they can to snuff out the dreams of those closest to them. They will us to believe that our goals are ridiculous and unattainable. While it's okay for them to have those opinions, we don't have to buy into them. We can grow in our awareness that we *are* the unusual ones. We can't expect most people to "get us". They think differently! They prefer to play it safe. It's comfortable for them. And while you may not prefer to identify yourself as "different", I can assure you, you are! How do I know? You are reading a book on how to release energetic money blocks! 😀

The sooner you accept your "weirdness", the faster you will grow! Part of that is refusing to apologize for your desires. Having them doesn't make you selfish. Give yourself the permission to think and **dream big**, unapologetically. And if you don't know how, you will learn in this chapter.

I know from experience how detrimental it can be to hold yourself back. For years, I didn't allow myself to want a nice place to live. I told myself that I already had so much, and that it would be selfish to want a nice home. I loved our condo in San Diego, but we had to sell it because it was getting to be too small for our growing family. We ended up leasing small apartment after small apartment because we couldn't make up our mind where we wanted to settle in at. During that time, we purchased cheap furniture, further instilling the feeling that it was all temporary. I wouldn't decorate or put in much effort, and my space definitely didn't feel like a *home*.

As I write this, we are on the way to Austin, Texas from the state of Washington. This time, it's going to be different. Because I am going to go ALL IN! I deserve to *love* where I live. And what we would love is to live in a house! I want a pool so that my children can happily swim. I want to live in a great school district. I want a beautiful, modern kitchen that regularly inspires my cooking. I desire an open-concept floorplan to be able to entertain and have magical dinners that build community. I look forward to sitting beside a fire-pit while having meaningful conversations with my husband. *And* I want a kid's play area so I can hear myself *think!* (Right, mommas?!) Above all, I want to create an experience for my family. For the past two years, my built-up shame and unworthiness blocked my heart from receiving that. Not anymore!

Built-up shame and unworthiness is also what creates the limiting money beliefs we carry. They are robbing us of experiences that our spirit craves, which in turn stunts the evolution of our existence. Even the smallest shift can lead you towards a vastly different destination. We will begin by diving into that shame and unworthiness and widening your perception. This will increase your confidence and open your heart to be willing to receive. Releasing money blocks also has tremendous side-benefits that will improve your spirituality, strengthen your connection with people, boost your creativity, enhance your physical health, and improve your daily habits.

The Four Main Money Beliefs

In the field of network marketing, many who participate transition from an "employee" model of income to an entrepreneurial model. An employee is someone who expects a specific amount of money for the hours they spend performing a task. An entrepreneur, on the other hand, is someone who will invest hours for little-to-no pay, knowing that the plentiful fruits of their labor will come later. For the transition from employee to entrepreneur to be successful, money blocks must be released.

The employee's framework of money creation is inherently limited. Why is this? Because the employee believes that their value is fixed on how much effort is exerted *per hour*. Since there is a limited number of hours in a day available to work, their value is limited. An entrepreneur's framework of money creation is based on creating value by *solving problems*. The more often that they can help someone solve a problem, the more compensation they receive. Their value isn't based on effort or time, it's based on how big of a problem they can solve, and how many people they can solve it for.

As Alonto and I mentor these budding entrepreneurs around the world, one of our discussions always revolves around their relationship with money. Observing their consistent and comparable struggles with finances, I have categorized the complaints into four types of money beliefs: **Morality, Scarcity, Competency** and **Environment**.

Each category has its own baseline frequency, and all of us have adopted a different variety of them. When working to release these money blocks, each category will have a specific protocol to accomplish. The more specific we are willing to get, the more effective the results will be. While one person may have the most issues with *morality* concerning money, another may have more surrounding their *competency* in how to create it. I personally had the most problems with *scarcity* and *competency*. It is also possible for someone to have a decent collection in all of the categories.

Morality

This category of beliefs represents shame and judgment of money. It is based on the belief that some people hold very near to their heart: *Money is evil and dirty. Those who have a lot of it are greedy. Having an abundance of money is bad. Being poor is good and humbling.* Movies often complement this belief. Characters with money are portrayed as corrupt, selfish and unkind. A financially successful person is rarely shown as the philanthropist and visionary.

Our physical body also adopts our mental and emotional beliefs. When a person's mentality is, *money is a bad thing,* they often can't even think about money without the chest constricting. As a result, money gets repelled. Think of it this way: when you have a closed, tight fist, what can enter into the palms of your hands? Nothing. In the same way, when your physical body tightens and tenses up while discussing money matters, the openness needed for money to flow is not there. That tension repels money instead of attracting it.

Another aspect of money shame is not feeling worthy enough to receive or manage wealth. Those that struggle with this have trouble even imagining themselves in the space to handle more money. They often say, *"I'm not good with money".* That statment emphasizes that they don't feel good enough to receive more money.

Shame encompasses the feeling of not being good enough or feeling like a bad person. It delivers an overall association that money is a bad thing. Shame is the lowest of the frequencies that the spirit can experience. It is the antithesis of who we truly are as a human. It is the opposite of unconditional love. When we feel *"money is evil"* regularly humming in the background, we carry the frequency of shame. As a result, we are seen as shameful.

What we claim about the outside world is merely a projection of our internal world. This is especially true when the emotions we are experiencing are *chronic* and *intense*. What is intensely felt about others or things (i.e. money), reveals how you feel about yourself.

Unworthiness dampens energy in all of your organs, meridians and chakras. It dulls the brilliance of your spirit. Unworthiness is insidious and spreads like a virus, replicating all throughout the system. It is the greatest contributor of stagnation and disease. A person who has taken the time and energy to release their shame is like a lit candle, with their inner flame burning brightly. But shame is like the candle snuffer that has the power to rob the flame of oxygen and completely deplete it. Vitality and vibrant energy come from knowing you are worthy of love and deserve to feel whole.

You deserve to feel good about money and receive what it is that you desire. It's time to repair and restore this relationship, which ultimately represents the relationship we have with ourselves. You are loved and more than enough. You are worthy and deserving of a healthy relationship with money. You deserve to experience your definition of success.

The next page features a list of money beliefs related to shame. Check off the ones that plague you. Take your time as you read each one. Check in with your body and heart. Remember, these feelings do not have to be screaming loud in your conscious mind to have a substantial effect. Most of the time they are subtle and quietly humming in the background, undetectable.

- [ ] Money is evil and dirty.
- [ ] It is greedy to have more than you need.
- [ ] Rich people are corrupt.
- [ ] I don't want life to be "all about money".
- [ ] I don't need a lot of money.
- [ ] I would rather give money away than receive it.
- [ ] I don't deserve to have a lot of money.
- [ ] I'm not worthy to receive more money.
- [ ] I'm not meant to make more money.
- [ ] It is selfish to have more than you need.
- [ ] Money doesn't make me happy.
- [ ] People will only want me for my money.
- [ ] More money will make me greedy and selfish.
- [ ] I should be happy with what I have.
- [ ] I'm not good with money.
- [ ] You can't be rich and spiritual.
- [ ] I would rather be happy than have money.
- [ ] Financial success isn't meant for me.
- [ ] Money is not important.
- [ ] I don't deserve nice things.
- [ ] I have a fear of success.
- [ ] I have a fear of failure.
- [ ] I'll lose my friends and family if I'm wealthy.

Scarcity

This category of money beliefs represents the perception that there is a shortage of money and resources. Anytime you say, *"I don't have enough _____",* you are demonstrating a scarcity mindset that needs to be shifted towards abundance. Catch yourself whenever you start your sentence that way. When we claim a lack of something, the brain and heart automatically see that as a truth instead of a problem. As a result, they stop looking for ways to improve and instead accept where you are as where you would like to be. Instead, it is best to ask yourself, *"How can I create more _____?"* or *"How can I afford _____?"* Those questions open the mind and heart to receive creative solutions.

Just as I shared that oxygen is abundantly available to all people on this planet to enjoy, money is also. The means to access it are all around us, but so often we are the ones causing the shortage. Imagine going to the doctor with a complaint of not being able to breathe well. The doctor enters the room and begins the assessment, only to discover that you have your nose plugged with your fingers! What would the doctor's advice be? *To unplug your nose!* Sometimes, I imagine God assesses our problems in the same way. How ridiculous for us to complain that there isn't enough, when the love and support to access more is overflowing all around us! We just need to get out of our own way and let go of what is causing our blocked flow.

There is still a "lizard brain" that exists in all of us. It is a primitive part of our brain, that alerts us of danger and ensures our survival. It is designed to protect us, *but* it has been known to take over and be hyperactive. It can fabricate all kinds of *"scary"* scenarios that keep us feeling unsafe and cause us to hide, performing below our capabilities. The lizard brain assigns most ideas as *harmful* and *dangerous.* Under its watchful eye, there is no room for creativity, innovation or opportunities.

The lizard brain isn't always wrong, though. There are legitimate dangers that it is accurate about, such as reminding us to avoid touching a hot stove or ensuring that we look both ways before walking into a busy street. A person in harmony allows the lizard brain to take over when it matters but also forces it to relax about the things that are not actually dangerous.

When it comes to money, the lizard brain tends to be hyperactive, because survival and money often go hand-in-hand. In order to calm the lizard brain, you have to create a whole-body experience of abundance. Instead of the nagging *not enough* syndrome you find yourself in that is validating the lizard brain, believe that all of your needs are met. True, you may actually be in a space of needing more money to pay off your pressing loans or bills. But in order to create the abundance you need, you first have to believe that it's yours. Strongly buy into the feeling that you have *more than enough* for an extended period of time, and it will appear.

This is possible because of the access of the Infinite that is available to you. You have access to all that is possible, including *more* and *plenty.* But attracting abundance requires more than an intellectual discussion. It requires a sense of certainty that you *are* abundant. You have to believe that it is true and feel it in your bones. That is what makes all the difference!

One way to begin making a lasting change is to be conscious of the language you are using on a regular basis. So often, we are using words that are detrimental to our belief systems and we aren't even aware that we're doing it! How often do you find yourself using the word *waste?* What an emotionally-charged word! When I was a child, I had it thrown in my face constantly.

"Stop *wasting* electricity!"

"Look at this moldy zucchini...what a *waste* of money!"

"This is such a *waste* of time!"

"Don't *waste* your money on that."

My mother is asian and grew up in poverty until the age of 16. It is understandable that she is frugal. Yet, she often takes it to the extreme. She will re-use an already used paper towel, multiple times, until you tell her that it's gross. One time, she got severe food poisoning because she ate fish that was left in the refrigerator for too long. Her reasoning stemmed from not wanting the fish to go to *waste*. But she ended up eating rotten food and hugged the porcelian bowl all night as a result! 🤮

My mother is a powerful money-creator, yet she still holds onto the idea of "don't waste anything, because one day you could end up with nothing". Being responsible and conscious of the earth's resources is one thing. But taking it to the extreme and eating legitamately expired foods because it would be wasteful to throw them away is pathological. If she were to release her traumatic past, the level of internal peace alone would be spectacular, let alone all of the liberated energy she would find herself with.

So I will ask again: is *waste* a word you often find in your vocabulary? It reflects a state of lack and reinforces that more will never come again. How horrifying! If love and healing is infinitely available, does the word *waste* even apply to our lives? We are eternal beings, yes? If we believe that, then how can we buy into the concept that we are *wasting* our time?

Sometimes a shift in perspective is all that you need. Ask yourself these questions,

"Do I have food to eat every day?"

"Do I have a place to sleep?"

"Are there people that love me?"

Yes, yes and *yes.*

"Am I currently experiencing my last breaths?"

No!

So, tell your lizard brain to **CALM DOWN**!

When you take a breath of oxygen that the earth has provided, do you follow it by saying, *"what a waste of oxygen..."* No way! Do you see how absurd that limited way of thinking really is? All around you, there is more than enough money, time, support, resources and creative solutions.

Awareness is always the first step. Begin to identify the

scarcity beliefs you struggle with by checking off the ones below that strike a chord within you.

- ☐ I don't have enough money.
- ☐ I can't afford it.
- ☐ I'll never have enough money.
- ☐ I'll never make more than I am making now.
- ☐ I'm going to run out of money.
- ☐ I'm afraid of losing what I have.
- ☐ I don't have time to make more money.
- ☐ I don't have the support I need.
- ☐ Money doesn't grow on trees.
- ☐ I often say: "It's too expensive".
- ☐ I avoid bills and pay at the latest possible date.
- ☐ I'm often late on payments.
- ☐ I stress when shopping for groceries.
- ☐ I'm afraid of outliving what I have.
- ☐ I am paranoid to spend money.
- ☐ I fear becoming ill and unable to make money.
- ☐ Once I earn it, I burn it.
- ☐ Money slips through my fingers.
- ☐ I'm holding my breath until my next paycheck.
- ☐ I just need to get through this month.
- ☐ I often say: "That's a waste of money".
- ☐ I often say: "That's a waste of time".

Competency

This category of money beliefs represents the skills, capability and confidence needed to create wealth. How do you feel about the strategies you are currently using to manage your money and increase your income? Do you feel confident that you are capable of mastering this "money game"? Or do you find yourself unable to get ahead because you are continually in a cycle of bad debt?

One thing I have learned is that money doesn't like to be bored. It either grows well when it is invested, or it finds a way to get spent. It is worth developing the necessary skills to create money flow and discern how to direct where it needs to go.

One considerable money block that Alonto and I encounter often in others is: *money is hard to make*. Many people fear that it will take too much time and effort to create more than what they currently have. They fail to realize that money isn't created through effort alone. It's created with energy. When you allow creative ideas to flow and trust in yourself, it is amazing to discover what is possible. It's even possible to create an entire day's worth of work in just one hour! When you find a way to deliver immense value to someone, the energetic exchange will be reciprocated. Value creation isn't dependent on more time per say, it's dependent upon results.

Let's say your car breaks down and you need to hire a mechanic. The first mechanic who you speak with is new to the industry, and he says, "This job is going to cost you

$500 and it will take me one week to get it done." But you are diligent in your research effort, so you also take your car to a skilled mechanic in the area for another quote. The second mechanic says, "This is an easy fix! It's going to cost you $500 and it will be ready for you by this evening!"

Which mechanic would you choose? It's the same cost for both, but one of them is the obvious choice. The second mechanic who was more skilled provided tremendous value by giving you more time with your car and less hassle overall. What if you had needed your car in order to take your kids to school or drive to work? If you had gone with the first mechanic, you would have needed to add the extra expense and trouble of acquiring a rental car. Saving a customer time is a HUGE value to offer. That's what Amazon and Uber are selling. They don't just offer a product/service, they are selling *time*.

In order to create significant value for others, you must first value yourself. Know that what you have to offer matters and is a meaningful contribution to society. When you feel and know these statements to be true, your reach and influence expands. On the other hand, insecurity leads to hesitant action or even inaction. Chronic and intense fear becomes a severe problem when it cripples, paralyzes, and keeps you from even starting a project. When and if you finally do start, the quality of the work is impacted greatly. There is a big difference between work that is produced with intense doubt than that which is produced with assurance. This doesn't mean that you shouldn't experience fear at all. You can still feel fear and courageously march on. Courage is not the absence of fear but proceeding in spite of it.

Confidence and certainty are needed in order to influence others. When someone is unsure of themselves and the product/service they provide, others are not motivated to purchase from them.

All purchasing decisions are emotional decisions.

As a customer, we want to feel confident that we are getting more value than what we are paying for. It is the seller's job to transfer that confidence.

Competency develops with mastery. Dedication to learning a skill means increasing the value that you can provide. I love how Naveen Jain, a billionaire entrepreneur, orders us to "forget about passion, think obsession." We have to have an *obsession* to solve a problem. The more you commit to the process of mastering a skill, the more that your value in the marketplace will continue to increase. It requires a dedication that is abnormal to the ordinary public. If this leads you to think, *"oh...* 😫 *...this is going to take a lot of time!"*, I can assure you that it doesn't have to be that way. An obsession is more than having fleeting enthusiasm for something. It is demonstrating a satisfying dedication and an insatiable curiosity to find out more. Believe me, you can do *so* much of that with just 1-2 hours a day!

One more important aspect of competency is knowing how to direct and manage money in the best way for you.

There are plenty of resources and mentors that exist that can help in this area. Understanding the role of energy exchange can also help you make healthier spending decisions. Every time you make a purchase, an energy exchange is taking place. Are you investing your dollars in places that don't belong? Are you *not* investing in places where it would be beneficial? How wonderful would it be to feel joyful and grateful every time you exchange money?! This could even be experienced for bills! Instead of looking at an electricity bill as a loss, you could see it as a gain! It's absolutely possible once you discern and direct the resources you have.

The protocols in the next chapter are designed to increase the emotional mastery needed to maintain growth in your work and business. It will help you to experience confidence and patience as you commit to your project or the development of a specific skill. Excessive doubt, fear and impatience is paralyzing and are major forms of distraction. You must learn how to change your state in order to stay focused on your important work.

Check off any of the following beliefs that you wrestle with often. You'll notice repeated beliefs in this category, as there are some beliefs that fall into more than one category.

- ☐ More money = more problems
- ☐ I'm not confident in myself.
- ☐ People don't listen to me when I make suggestions.
- ☐ I'm too old.
- ☐ I'm too young
- ☐ I don't believe that I can do _____.

- ☐ I don't know how to create money.
- ☐ Money is hard to make.
- ☐ To make more money, I would have to work very hard and be in the grind.
- ☐ It takes too much time to make money.
- ☐ I don't want to take time away from my family to make money.
- ☐ I'll never make enough.
- ☐ I don't know how to manage money.
- ☐ I won't know what to do with more money.
- ☐ I'm not good with money.
- ☐ I don't want the responsibility that comes with money.
- ☐ I keep getting into debt.
- ☐ I can't seem to get financially settled.
- ☐ I don't have any mentors to teach me how to become wealthy.
- ☐ I am disorganized and scattered.
- ☐ I am not creative enough.
- ☐ I don't believe in myself; I have a lot of self-doubt.
- ☐ Money is too complicated.
- ☐ I don't have any income-producing skills.
- ☐ I don't have a business mind.
- ☐ I'm not good at sales.

Environment

A cactus grows well in the desert, but not in the rainforest. A palm tree grows well in the tropics, but not in the mountains. Just like plants require the appropriate environment to thrive, so does a human being. The people we surround ourselves with, our mentors, our homes and offices, our land, the food we eat, the books we read, the podcasts we listen to, the music we play, the movies we watch: all of these are continuously affecting our energetic flow. We don't live in a vacuum. It is inevitable that we adapt to the beliefs and attitudes of the people we hang out with and the content we consume, especially if one is not extremely confident and certain in who they are and what they represent. Add that to the intended and unintended conditioning of our parents' beliefs and attitudes about money (and life) we take on. That is a lot of energetic conditioning!

Do you have aspects of your personality you know is an exact replica of your mom or dad? Perhaps you don't like that particular aspect, but you're not sure how to change. Rest assured, you can release the aspects of yourself that aren't serving your highest good. No matter how difficult your childhood was, you can persevere and rise above the conditions you grew up in. It is possible to use our struggles as fuel to drive us into growth.

All that you are physically exposed to influences your frequencies. External details serve as triggers to guide you in a direction that is either more or less in alignment with your truth. Design environments that support your expansion. Let go of things that do not hold a purpose or give you immense joy (thank you, Marie Kondo!). A home filled with clutter and disarray will surely distract you from inspired execution. When you rearrange your physical space, energy flow shifts. That change will in-turn rearrange how energy flows in your meridians. What is done on the physical level affects the soul, and vice versa. Body, mind and spirit are one. No matter what angle you choose to focus on, the others will be affected. Let's be efficient and up-level the most we can by working on our energy body and our physical environment.

Check off all of the environmental reasons why money creation is a challenge:

- ☐ I'm not doing well because of the economy.
- ☐ Taxes are killing me.
- ☐ It's the government's fault; I blame those in office.
- ☐ Our family is not good with money.
- ☐ My spouse/partner is the reason why we aren't getting ahead.
- ☐ My parents were always worried about money and I learned from them.
- ☐ We had just enough to get by in my childhood, so now I earn just enough to get by.
- ☐ I wasn't born into money.
- ☐ I don't have time to make more money; my schedule is already packed.
- ☐ My friends are holding me back.

- ☐ My parents weren't responsible with money and neither am I.
- ☐ My parents struggled with finances, and so do I.
- ☐ I'm overwhelmed and do not know where to start.
- ☐ I never had great role models and mentors to teach me about money.
- ☐ The rich get richer and the poor get poorer.
- ☐ The city/neighborhood I live in is holding me back.
- ☐ My kid(s) are holding me back.
- ☐ My home is overwhelming to me, and I can't think straight.
- ☐ My office is disorganized.
- ☐ I can't create more income, because all that my family and I have ever done is _____ and I don't want to disappoint them.
- ☐ I am comfortable with where I am at; embarking on something new is intimidating.
- ☐ I don't have the support I need.
- ☐ I am physically not able to make money.

You did it!

Look through the four checklists and observe which category (or categories) stand out the most. That will help to bring awareness to your current money story. Awareness is the first step to up-leveling!

[CHAPTER 6]

Money and Me

This chapter is about to be written by _you_. It will contain the money story that you have been carrying for your entire life. Does the idea of that make you nervous? Good! This is a necessary part of the process. Writing can reveal truths that otherwise get left unnoticed. By putting pen to paper, you have the capacity to gain insight into what has been defining you for so long. It's important that you are willing to get raw and honest as you dive deeply into all of the details that you can possibly think of.

DO NOT SKIP THIS CHAPTER!

It _must_ be completed before continuing on to ensure that you get the very best results.

A great way to start is by chronologically writing down what you can remember from your childhood. Dig into your parents' (or guardians') attitudes towards money. Recall what their spending habits were like and how they operated their finances. What common phrases about money were repeated often while you were growing up? Once your childhood is captured, transition into the memories from your teenage years. Finally, write about your experiences as an adult, including *everything* that you think and feel about your complicated relationship with money. If you happen to get stuck, refer to the previous chapter and expand upon the items that you selected.

Please do not hesitate to write here in this book. This is a sacred space that has been created for you and it has the potential to hold the space for healing your relationship with money and ultimately yourself, should you allow it. You deserve to release the pain and gain valuable insight into your personal money makeup.

Wasn't that cathartic?! Did you notice which category of money beliefs you had the most? It was important that we finished this exercise first so that you can customize your protocols in the next chapter. For example, if you have more limiting beliefs and heavy emotional ties concerning *scarcity* and *environment*, then you can apply the protocols for only those sections. But, if you are an overachiever like me, then you may tackle all of the categories. 😊

[CHAPTER 7]

R + R: Release and Renew

It's the moment you have been waiting for! It is finally time for you to transform your energetic patterns and design a brand-new lifestyle! I am extremely excited for you! 😍 In this chapter, we will be applying essential oils and performing exercises for each category of limiting money beliefs. You may choose to apply all of the protocols or just the ones that are the most applicable to your specific money makeup.

I recommend completing the protocol for the *environment* category no matter what your particular money blocks are, though. It's safe to assume that you have adopted difficult generational beliefs about money, as so many of us have. Plus, there are always improvements that can be made in your physical environment. This includes anything from your physical location, the people that you surround yourself with, and even how you have chosen to organize your home or office.

Let's release the old, destructive energies that you have held about money for so long. After that, we will renew ourselves with an elevated and nourishing vibration. All of the elements of *clear, nourish* and *harmonize* are within each section. After a protocol, you may feel like a huge weight has been lifted off of your body and your heart. You'll finally be able to take in a deep, soothing and life-giving breath.

It would do you well to refresh yourself on the possible side effects that we outlined earlier. Waves of emotions, crying spells, fits of rage, and even emotional numbness can occur as you progress through these protocols. Have confidence in the fact that these are only temporary and are a part of releasing the energetic ties you have held. Give yourself grace and understanding for 24 hours after a protocol, so that your body may ease into your new rhythm.

Here are some **basic instructions** for the protocols:

- Only apply one protocol per day.

- You may choose to complete the protocol in each category only once, or you may repeat the same protocol for a few consecutive days. For example: You may choose to apply the *"morality"* protocol once a day, for three days straight. On Day 4, you may choose to switch and complete the *"scarcity"* protocol. Finally, on Day 5, maybe you decide to apply the protocol for your *"environment"*. All of this is an acceptable way to progress through the different categories. Listen to your intuition for the answer to how many days a protocol needs to be repeated. This is a very personal journey.

- A good general guideline is to complete one category protocol for three consecutive days.

- Seven days is the maximum recommended length of time to repeat a category protocol.

- You may choose to apply each of the four category protocols during four consecutive days (only one per day), and then repeat the entire process again. For example:

  > Day 1: Morality
  >
  > Day 2: Scarcity
  >
  > Day 3: Competency
  >
  > Day 4: Environment

  If this is the method that you choose, do not repeat the process more than five times.

- You can skip a day (or even more in some cases) in-between the categories if you need more time to process the changes.

- After completing a round of all of the categories that you want, this entire process may be revisited again. This can be especially helpful when you are hitting a ceiling in your finances. If you aren't pleased, start it back up again!

- Each application can be done at any time of the day. Again, trust your intuition.

- Make sure to drink extra water, move your body, go outside, take an epsom salt bath, and rest when necessary. These are all excellent ways to help with the detox process.

- Journal, Journal, Journal. Write and document what you are going through. This is a phenomenal way to assist you with processing while you are in the moment and also for tracking your progress.

Morality

This section may be the most challenging. As we dive into shame, there are sure to be moments that are unpleasant. You must choose to meet it face-to-face in order to release it. You do not need to have focused thoughts while applying the essential oil protocol. Allow the oils to do the heavy lifting. All that is required from you is to apply the oils and breathe.

Copaiba: This essential oil binds and attaches to the frequency of shame. It dislodges it from all of the organs, meridians and chakras, as well as any part of you that has been tormented with feelings of inadequacy and feeling like you're not enough. Copaiba absorbs those frequencies into its rich, thick resin, like a dry sponge does for water. It has an affinity to attract unworthiness vibrations. Applying it to the bottoms of the feet maximizes foot reflexology. It allows the oil to access every part of your body without having to physically bathe in it. 😜

Lemongrass: This essential oil must be paired with Copaiba for the complete release of shame. It's flavor is acrid and spicy, which means it has the ability to disperse stagnant energy effectively. Once Copaiba has bound up those

Morality Protocol

1. **Copaiba:** APPLY A THIN LAYER ALL OVER THE BOTTOMS OF THE FEET

2. **Lemongrass:** APPLY I DROP ON THE HEART

3. **Siberian Fir:** USE AS MUCH AS NEEDED TO APPLY A THIN LAYER DOWN THE SPINE AND SACRUM

4. **Pink Pepper:** APPLY I DROP ON THE 3RD EYE CENTER. INHALE THE AROMA FROM THE HANDS FOR 3 MINS

5. **Rose:** ROLL INSIDE OF THE ELBOW CREASES AND OVER THE LOWER ABDOMEN

shame frequencies, lemongrass then disperses it, much like an ignited firework. By applying it on the heart, we are not only unwinding the chest, but also touching all of the organs. This is due to the fact that the heart rules all of the organs in Traditional Chinese Medicine (TCM).

Siberian Fir: This is a supportive oil that soothes out the intense release of copaiba and lemongrass. It restores smooth circulation of Qi in the lungs. The lungs are responsible for maintaining unobstructed circulation of Qi around the body.

Pink Pepper: This essential oil strengthens the throat and heart chakras, to improve the words that are spoken. Pink pepper helps you carefully choose words that reflect your divine nature. It brings awareness to the power of what you say regularly, so that you speak with precise intention.

Rose: This flower oil is nourishing and harmonizing. It is supportive to the siberian fir and pink pepper, providing the undertone of unconditional love and self-respect. Rose reflects gentleness, beauty and grace. It helps you to be kinder to yourself and highlight all that you are doing right. One other aspect of rose is that it brings excitement to the heart for what is to come and a gratitude for the transformations taking place right now. Application to the lower abdomen allows access to Ren 6, or the Sea of Qi, which instills the frequencies of worthiness and self-love. Ren 6 fosters your original Qi and tonifies the kidneys, which means that it assists in building up your core essence. It is the foundation of all yin and yang energies in the body. You will rise up, feeling strong in who you are and what you are capable of.

Scarcity

Are you tired of the angst you feel about money? Worrying if you'll have enough with every purchase and expense? Maintaining these feelings only generates more scarcity. I'm excited for you to feel joy and freedom in your finances! Regardless of the state of your bank account and liabilities you have on paper, you have the right to feel abundant in your spirit right now.

Marjoram: This essential oil has a dual role of cleansing and calming. It targets the anxious and unsettled frequency that is erratic and volatile. It helps to expel the grief and despair that comes along with living in a state of scarcity. Marjoram supports the spleen by unwinding *worry* and *overthinking* that knots the Qi. It then soothes the lungs by restoring proper lung Qi flow. The lungs are responsible for releasing the old (carbon dioxide) and inspiring the new (oxygen). If this flow is impeded, too much *old* builds up and not enough *new* is received. When the body is starving for oxygen, the spirit feels like it's suffocating, which causes the emotional response of "not enough".

Tea Tree: This essential oil introduces the "clean-up crew" to take care of any of the volatile residue that was left behind from the marjoram application. From time-to-time, I will incorporate a secondary cleansing essential oil to ensure residual unwanted energies have shifted. The inside of the elbow crease has the lung, pericardium and heart

Scarcity Protocol

1. *Marjoram*: APPLY 2 DROPS ACROSS THE UPPER CHEST

2. *Tea Tree*: APPLY A LAYER INSIDE BOTH OF THE ELBOW CREASES

3. *Lemongrass*: APPLY 1-2 DROPS AROUND BOTH OF THE WRISTS

4. *Spikenard* + *Wild Orange* + *Roman Chamomile*:
   MIX TOGETHER AND RUB ALL OVER THE BELLY + SACRUM.
   INHALE THE AROMA FROM THE HANDS FOR 3 MINUTES

5. *Patchouli*: APPLY A THIN LAYER ON THE BOTTOMS OF THE FEET

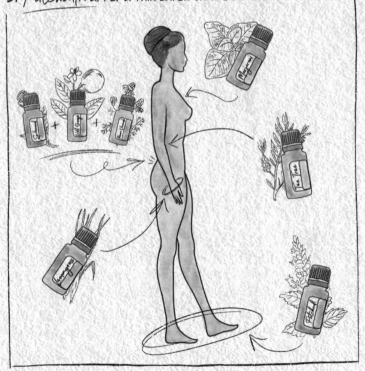

channels passing through. This is my favorite application point for releasing tension in the chest.

Lemongrass: This essential oil pairs with and is supportive to the marjoram in expelling anxious energies. Marjoram is the initial cleanser. Lemongrass takes that bound-up energy that the marjoram pushed out and disintegrates it into the atmosphere. It transforms the jagged frequency into a neutral frequency, so that the energy has the potential to be transformed into something better.

Spikenard + Wild Orange + Roman Chamomile: The brilliant combination of these three essential oils transmits sacred energy from the Divine. It creates a feeling of oneness and connection. It is nearly impossible to feel alone and isolated using this combination. Applying this trio on the abdomen amplifies the feeling of unity between you and all that is around you. The solar plexus in particular holds a point, Ren 12, that means "between Heaven and Earth". It is the center-point between our physical self and the heavens. Spikenard and wild orange together amplify the transmission of Divine love, and transcends the ordinary experiences of daily living. Roman chamomile then acts as the interpreter, helping us to put the received wisdom and guidance into words and visions.

Patchouli: This essential oil is used to harmonize and integrate the entire protocol, so that the body receives and physically feels the sensation of unity and abundance. It helps you feel rooted, safe and secure.

Competency

You are more competent than you realize. Take mother-hood, for example. Most moms don't identify with having a large skill-set, but it couldn't be further from the truth! Being a mother comes with many valuable skills that translate over in the marketplace: the art of persuasion, organization, listening, problem-solving and commitment, just to name a few. A change in perspective allows you to take the skills you already possess, master them and take ownership in the value you provide. From there, you can continue to expand upon your abilities through practice and dedication.

Cal Newport, author of *Deep Work,* often says that work satisfaction (soul satisfaction) comes from mastery. It takes the discipline of focus and follow-through to achieve mastery in whatever you desire. That means you must also take your personal distractions into account and acknowledge where and when you are not in alignment. This next protocol allows you to flush out your doubts and insecurities, leaving confidence for your choices and the ability to deliver your gift to humanity.

Lavender: This essential oil brings insecurities and doubts to the surface, in an effort to assist the rest of the oils to release them. It does have some energetic clearing abilities, however, it needs the support of other essential oils to complete the clearing action. In TCM, every organ is linked to particular emotions. When lavender enters the lungs, heart and kidneys, it touches on the sorrow, sadness and fears/doubts that those organs store.

Competency Protocol

1. *Lavender*: APPLY 2 DROPS TO HANDS AND INHALE FOR 2 MINUTES

2. *Cypress*: APPLY TO THE LIVER 14 ACUPUNCTURE POINT (ALONG THE BRA LINE)

3. *Coriander*: APPLY TO THE STOMACH CHANNEL OF THE LOWER LEG

4. *Bergamot* + *Green Mandarin* + *Wild Orange*:

   MIX 1 DROP OF EACH TOGETHER AND RUB ON THE SOLAR PLEXUS; INHALE THE AROMA FROM THE HANDS FOR 2 MINUTES

5. *Frankincense*: APPLY TO THE BOTTOMS OF THE FEET

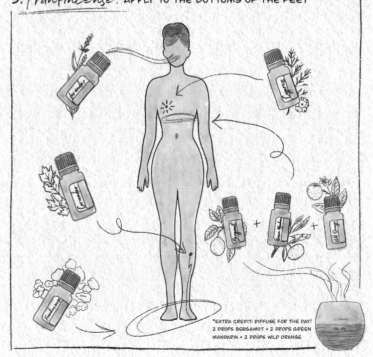

*EXTRA CREDIT: DIFFUSE FOR THE DAY! 2 DROPS BERGAMOT + 2 DROPS GREEN MANDARIN + 2 DROPS WILD ORANGE

Cypress: This essential oil pairs well with lavender for releasing old, trapped emotions. Cypress is known to be one of the most powerful Qi movers, like a large cement-drill breaking through concrete. When applied to the Liver 14 acupuncture point, its effects are multiplied. Liver is the General of Qi, and overlooks the smooth flow of it throughout all of the organs. Cypress applied in this location ensures the release of the doubts, fears and insecurities that are held within all of them.

Coriander: This essential oil enters and soothes the stomach and spleen, helping us to feel at home with ourselves. This pair of organs are a part of the Earth Element, which represent Mother Earth. The earth gives us a "sense of belonging and a sense of home. When we have the power of the Earth Element, we can feel at peace within ourselves because we are grounded and balanced (Worsley, 38)". Applying coriander helps us to feel at home with ourselves. It provides a foundation for seeds of self-confidence and self-acceptance to grow and thrive.

Bergamot + Green Mandarin + Wild Orange: I call this the *Courageous Trio*. This powerhouse combination enables you to rise up with confidence in yourself and believe that you are capable of learning a new skill. If you've doubted yourself before, this trio encourages your soul to take that leap and commit to mastering better money habits as well as high-income-producing activities. Bergamot provides the encouragement to enable you to believe "this is possible for me". Green mandarin opens the heart to receive this higher version of yourself and gives you the drive to carry it through. Wild orange is the gift that keeps on giving, so you feel an abundance of resources and energy that is available to you at any time.

Frankincense: This is our harmonizing essential oil that ties the protocol together, making sure it sticks and that the new frequencies integrate effectively into your system. Frankincense is an amplifier. Stubborn patterns of self-doubt, insecurity and fear need the extra boost from Frankincense to ensure transformation. It is also grounding and assists you to stand in your power.

Environment

Have you ever questioned your beliefs? Have you ever sincerely wanted to change them but did not know how? Every belief comes with an emotion, and every emotion comes with a particular frequency. When you change the frequency, you change the belief. If you want to change the music on the radio, all you have to do is change the channel (frequency). As you apply the next protocol, imagine you are changing your personal dial to hear a brand-new tune!

Note: If you have the ability, go outside and stand barefoot on the earth for five minutes right after applying this protocol. It would be even better to do the entire protocol outside. It helps to drain the energy back into the earth.

Wintergreen: This essential oil helps us to finally be open to letting go of the old story we have identified with. It is more of a gentle nudge rather than a harsh stripping. Wintergreen softens the heart and opens the mind to let go, so that the shift doesn't feel as abrupt. The top of the head is

Environment Protocol

1. **Wintergreen**: APPLY TO THE TOP OF THE HEAD

2. **Lemongrass**: APPLY TO THE TOPS OF THE SHOULDERS, BOTH SIDES

3. **Tumeric**: APPLY DOWN THE SPINE

4. **Siberian Fir + Peppermint**: MIX THE OILS TOGETHER IN THE HAND AND INHALE THE AROMA FOR 3 MINUTES

5. **Indian Sandawood**: APPLY TO THE BOTTOMS OF THE FEET

6. **Green Mandarin**: APPLY TO THE TOP OF THE HEAD

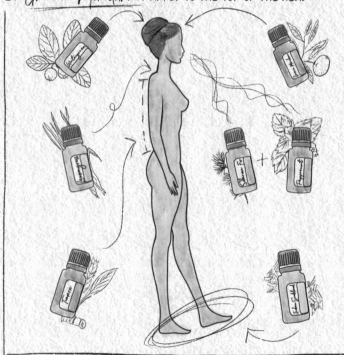

a wonderful location to swiftly circulate an essential oil all throughout the body.

Lemongrass: This essential oil unravels the toxic belief systems that enslave and destroy the expression of one's soul. This is especially true for those particular beliefs that have been held since childhood. Lemongrass has the remarkable ability to find the most harmful frequencies that impede flow and easily liberates the energy for better use. The tops of the shoulders is where the Gall Bladder 21 acupuncture point is located, which descends and drains Qi down from the head. *(Note: If pregnant, please skip this step.)*

Tumeric: This essential oil is pungent and bitter in flavor. The pungent flavor breaks-up stagnation with vigorous movement of Qi while the bitter elements drain toxicity downward. Tumeric supports the lemongrass in this way to drain toxic energies. On a physical level, tumeric is known to slow the proliferation of cancer cells. Hence, it pinpoints the malignant type of energies and inhibits their continued growth. I use this essential oil when it's time to purge intensely difficult patterns. Consider this oil one of your strongest weapons for resistance to change.

Siberian Fir + Peppermint: These essential oils open the lungs and move liver Qi. This is the breath of fresh air after all of the hard work of clearing from the oils above. They are supportive and encouraging, assuring you that you are doing the right thing. They also help to restore the proper rhythm and flow of Qi after experiencing major shifts. After a dam breaks, the initial surge of water is extreme. This can be comparable to how it feels after immense clearing and release. Siberian fir and peppermint help to calm the surge into a manageable flow.

Indian Sandalwood + Green Mandarin: These are the harmonizing essential oils. They help to ground in this new pattern you are experiencing. The goal is to make this up-level your new normal and prevent self-sabotage from ensuing. Indian sandalwood opens sacred connection with the Divine, so that you may receive guidance from a holy place. Sandalwood sedates the lizard brain and activates your inner wisdom. Green mandarin greatly assists in opening the heart to receive this divine connection and the new blessings into your life. There is always some kind of blessing waiting to be received, but it requires an open heart to take it in.

Once you have finished all of the categories you feel are beneficial to you during this season in your life, consider diffusing some of these blends for a few days. It will continue the beautiful momentum you have generated from the work you have completed.

Diffuser Blends

Place two drops of each in your favorite diffuser.

Douglas Fir + Wild Orange + Lime

Spikenard + Lime + Lemon

Ginger + Lemon + Cypress

Spikenard + Juniper Berry + Lime

Douglas Fir + Frankincense + Lemon

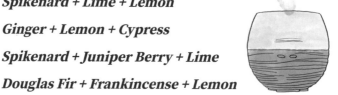

Continue to this next section once you are finished completing the protocols.

My dear friend, you are glowing in your new energies and they look great on you! Your outlook on yourself, your life and money has shifted! This is the perfect time for *Abundance Affirmations.*

This free flow of energy that you have created is the perfect condition to receive and cultivate these new beliefs. For the longest time, you have been listening to your inner-critic. I now want to challenge you to listen to your inner-encourager. A great way to accomplish this is to open the voice-recording application of your phone and record yourself reading these powerful, life-giving statements. You can then listen to yourself proclaiming greatness every day as a part of your meditation practice.

It might feel silly at first, but your subconscious mind is listening and integrating what you say. This is why it is best to hear your voice instead of someone else's. There is no one out there that you trust more than yourself. It is possible to enhance the recording and make it even more powerful. Simply add high-frequency music in the background! There are plenty of tracks to choose from on YouTube.

This kind of practice is what has made me the healer that I am today. For most of my medical practice, I didn't believe in myself and lacked the confidence in my ability as an effective practitioner. Listening to my personal voice recording every day is what developed my confidence and was instrumental in the creation of my first book, *I am Fabulous.*

You can use the statements below or design your own! Think of yourself as a blank canvas with an infinite number of possibilities. It is up to you to paint your canvas how you would like it to look.

Abundance Affirmations

I am so happy and grateful now that _____.

I deeply and completely love and accept all that I am.

I am worthy and deserving of love and healing.

I have love flowing through me constantly.

I am provided for in every way.

I have all of the things I need and want.

Money flows to me easily and abundantly.

There is more than enough money available for me.

I deserve to earn as much money as I choose.

I am great at managing money and I know how to direct it.

I provide immense value to the people around me.

Others respect and see my worth.

The more value I provide, the more money I attract.

I am continually learning how to provide more value.

I am so grateful for all the money I receive and the ability to take care of my needs and wants.

I listen to my truth and continually align with my inner wisdom.

I make decisions that create energetic flow and expansion.

I am confident in myself and am certain of the decisions I make.

I trust myself and the direction I am going.

I have more than enough resources available to me.

I have more than enough ideas, people, talent and time to achieve my goals.

I regularly attract opportunities that are in alignment with my vision.

I receive abundance easily.

I am so happy and grateful now that I am a Money Magnet!

[CHAPTER 8]

Move to the Beat

You, like every person on this earth, were given a sacred song to play in this lifetime. It is an expression of your Soul and it *begs* for you to move to its beat so that the world may be impacted by its beautiful melody.

Have you ever been emotionally-moved from watching a graceful dancer? I have. I love witnessing the pure magic in their interpretation of the music. I watch entranced as they move through each note, pausing when appropriate, leaping at the crescendo and creating an overall masterful experience. Its supernatural and transcendent, not only for the dancer, but for everyone watching as well. On the other hand, I've also witnessed the opposite. When a dancer is off-beat, its excruciating to watch. My face cringes and my body contracts. It's painful to witness.

What impact have you had on your audience? Are you on beat with the rhythm of your soul? Or are you missing your cues and causing everyone to look away?

Alonto and I are Salsa and West Coast Swing dancers. We have learned so much about the rhythm in songs as a result. Every song has an up-beat and a down-beat. It plays throughout the entire song and can be identified in the "boom...chic...boom...chic...boom...chic". When dancing, every beat gets accentuated by a move or a pause. Both are equally important and impactful. They just have to be timed and executed appropriately.

It's the same with surfing! A surfer doesn't paddle to the shore at just *any* time. He/she paddles vigorously when a wave is coming and pops up on their surfboard when the wave is starting to break. This gives them the longest and most satisfying ride. Reading the water and timing the paddle and pop-up make all the difference for a gratifying surf.

How is your timing? Nature naturally reflects the cycles of yin and yang everywhere. Yang is found in the activity: the movement, execution, and creation. It's nature's up-beat. Yin is the pause, rest, reflection, and nourishment. It's the down-beat. It is critical to be in-tune with your cycles. When you flow with your season, life feels effortless. You catch the metaphorical wave of a yang cycle and rest with a yin cycle. The way to make life "hard" is to go against your cycles. Energy stagnates when you procrastinate during a time that is designated for activity. Energy drains when you are active during a season intended for rest. Flow in your cycles to maximize growth and create energetic flow. A simple way to discern your cycles can be accomplished through this:

Listen to your intuition.

Move to the beat of your soul's rhythm to release emotional stagnations and generate energy flow in your meridians and chakras.

Be Decisive

Masterful decision-making is both an art and a skill that can be developed. The root-word *cis* means "to cut" and *de* means "off". When we make a decision, we are making a choice and "cutting off" all other possibilities.

We live in a field of infinite choices. It is only through the act of cutting off the experiences that we prefer not to have that the infinite can be narrowed down into one specific outcome. The more clear we are with what we want, the more energy surges through to manifest that which we desire. When we are unsure, doubtful, hesitant, or even stuck between two options, the focus becomes diluted and manifesting the favorable outcome will either slow down or not happen at all.

Swift and confident decision-making is a skill you must master in order to truly live in alignment. It requires listening, discerning and executing bravely. The better you are at it, the easier the manifestation process will happen. The overall quality of your life will multiply exponentially as you learn to prevent the agony of indecision.

Many fear making a decision because they have been led to believe that there is always a right and a wrong choice. That theory gets messy and complicated, though, when life proves that it doesn't operate according to a black-

and-white rule book. The worst thing that you can do is stay in limbo for extended periods of time. There is an energy drainage that comes along with it. Opportunities for focused creation are missed during that valuable time. Committing to a decision, even if it ends up taking you down a path that you realize you'd rather not see-through, gives you feedback and a depth of understanding that remaining stuck in limbo never could offer. Therefore, being indecisive creates more stagnation than making a "wrong decision" ever could.

The skill of making confident decisions is vital to a successful relationship with money. Every day we are making purchasing decisions. Majority of them, I'm sure, are ones you give little-to-no conscious thought to. We buy with our emotions. Excessive fear, sadness, anger, grief and worry all contribute to sub-optimal and regretful purchasing decisions. They push us towards fast and cheap products and services instead of quality ones with substantial value. But we can change that! Your purchases have the power to be made consciously and intentionally based on the quality products and services that you are excited to consume!

You can and should be aware of where you invest your dollars. Every purchase at a store or business is an exchange of energy. Whether you are purchasing food or shoes or dish soap, would you call it a high-quality energy exchange? As I have learned to value myself, I have learned to value only the best quality things in life, because I am worthy and deserving of it! And so are you! You deserve to have quality products in your home, quality relationships around you, quality time spent throughout your day, and definitely high-quality essential oils to use! 😊 This book is a great start to your quest for quality. There are multiple tools included to massively up-level the way you operate and deal with life's challenges. No matter what struggles come our way, they can be handled with wisdom and grace. It's time to get into alignment with your higher Self, beyond the ego, and make your life a masterpiece!

Soul Rhythm Protocol

Your intuition is in-tune with the rhythm of your soul. Trusting and following it is always the answer for how to make the best decisions. But how is that done? Easy! I've put together the following protocol for you to use whenever you are feeling misaligned or unsure of the direction you want to go. The answers are within you, you just need to learn to access them.

Applying this protocol is a two-fold process. The first step will raise the volume of your higher Self so that you can distinctly hear the messages that you need to hear. The second step guides you to trust in yourself. This is necessary to ensure we break through those stubborn inner conflicts of yours. 😄 At times, you may receive a message loud and clear, but still question its validity. To act in confidence, you have to expand your feelings of trust. Once that is completed, you will have no excuse but to follow through on what matters to your Soul. This protocol can be used at anytime in your life, even outside of releasing money blocks. It can even be applied once a day, if needed. For optimal results, apply it at the beginning of the day, so that you may evaluate its effects by the end of the day.

Soul Rhythm Protocol

1. *Lemongrass:* APPLY ONE DROP AROUND THE BELLY BUTTON

2. *Roman Chamomile:* APPLY TO SAN JIAO 18 (BEHIND THE EAR ON THE MASTOID PROCESS

3. *Coriander:* APPLY ACROSS THE DIAPHRAGM

4. *Clary Sage* + *Patchouli* + *Douglas Fir:*
   MIX ONE DROP OF EACH IN THE HANDS AND INHALE THE AROMA FOR THREE MINUTES

Lemongrass: This essential oil is used to bring about awareness and to clear what is not in alignment with your core essence. Sometimes we go along participating in things not because it provides purpose or value in our lives, but simply because that's what we are used to doing. Lemongrass provides an *"a-ha!"* experience by showing you what is destructive and no longer nourishing. This might even include friendships or partnerships. The belly button is my favorite location to energetically circulate an essential oil quickly all over the body.

Roman Chamomile: This essential oil calms a very specific kind of anxiousness. It is the kind of anxiety that overwhelms the body when a radical change needs to take place in your life and it scares you to even think about it. Marianne Williamson's famous quote captures the kind of anxiety that Roman chamomile has the ability to alleviate:

> "OUR DEEPEST FEAR IS NOT THAT WE ARE inadequate.
>
> OUR DEEPEST FEAR IS THAT WE ARE
>
> powerful beyond measure.
>
> IT IS OUR light, NOT OUR DARKNESS,
>
> THAT MOST FRIGHTENS US."
>
> —Marianne Williamson

The San Jiao 18 application point behind the ear calms fright and improves your ability to hear messages.

Coriander: This essential oil applied on the diaphragm guides you towards being in resonance with your cycles, just as it regulates the inhale and exhale of the lungs. The lungs regulate both the inspiration of the new and the release of the old. Coriander assists your body to take in fresh, nourishing Qi and exhale that which no longer serves you.

Clary Sage + Patchouli + Douglas Fir: Both nourishing and harmonizing, this combination provides insight, acceptance and implementation. Lemongrass pointed out what was not working, while clary sage reveals to you what *is* working and what *will* work for you in the future. Patchouli helps you accept the truths that are revealed, so that you do not ignore or deny them. Douglas fir gives you momentum to follow through with those truths.

Using your *Values Compass* from Chapter 4 provides a *logical* way to make decisions, while the *Soul Rhythm* protocol is a way for your emotional body to make decisions. Your entire body will either expand or contract when presented with an option. This can be used for planning your days and weeks, too!

Space Clearing

There is a part of me that secretly wants to be a Feng Shui expert. 😊 While I can't necessarily go into all of the minute details of where to place items in your home, I am fully aware of how much a person's physical space reflects their energetic state. It also deeply influences their energy. This is why it is critical to regularly purge your home of what is not necessary. Donating, gifting, or even dumping items that neither bring you joy nor have practical use yield the greatest amounts of energetic flow. Rearranging your home even has the power to rearrange your emotions!

Your things have a frequency, too! It is important to have things surrounding you that uplift and expand your vibrations. I often ask students in my workshops, "What is the music of your home?" Your home is certainly playing something, because every time you walk in, you are greeted with certain feelings. The home is a sacred place for us to restore our spirit. It is our personal sanctuary. Does your home provide you with a space to recover after battling the world all day?

Set up your home for maximum healing and recovery. A simple diffuser blend from my *I am Fabulous* book is "Clear the Clutter". Tried and true, the clutter gets cleared when this blend is diffused!

Can you tell how much I love **lemongrass**?! This oil in combination with **douglas fir** brings up intense feelings of disgust for the things that you don't need in your home. It's as if you can't get rid of it fast enough! Like a metal detector beeps when it hovers over metal, your body will beep when your eyes come across an item that has to go. **Lime** gets you excited for the changes that you are creating, in an effort for you to keep up with the progress and not give up too soon. *Warning: don't diffuse this before bed! You'll be up all night clearing, cleaning and organizing.*

Another side benefit of "Clear the Clutter" is that it taps into your intuition to set up your home for maximum energy flow. It's an added bonus after the *Soul Rhythm* protocol has enhanced your ability to know what's right for you. You'll know how to arrange items and what to keep out on counters/shelves, so that your home triggers healthy habits and behaviors. For my family, that means we always have our diffuser and essential oils out, as well as a juicer and a yoga mat. Being able to see them everyday makes us use them more often.

Lastly, perhaps "clearing the clutter" for you means more than just sorting through the items *inside* of your home. Maybe it means moving them into a totally different one! If your body reacts to that statement, then you know that this message is meant for you. This topic is very near and dear to me, because I have personally learned the importance of living in the right neighborhood, in the right city, at the right time. I have also witnessed too many people remain in a home that they hate, simply because they feared change and the unknown. They believed moving would be a major financial hassle because of the amount of possessions that they own. While I do understand that moving can be stressful, I also have personally discovered the cost of living somewhere that doesn't resonate with you.

It is way more expensive in the long run. Make the effort to move somewhere that makes you happy! Your energy changes with your physical environment. Every country, every city, every neighborhood has its own pulse. Make sure that your soul beats to the rhythm of where you are. When there is harmony between you and your physical space, achieving energetic flow is easier, and your soul's music is amplified. An amplified soul easily translates magnetic energy to financial abundance!

Receive Well

If you want to earn well, you must learn to receive well. Giving is yang and receiving is yin. There are so many ways in which you demonstrate how great of a giver you are: you listen to your friend vent about a crisis they are experiencing. You babysit your nieces/nephews for your sister so that she can have some time to herself. You take your mom to her doctor's visits. And you regularly take care of your home for your family to enjoy. In the give and receive cycle, most of us are excellent givers. But we need help in the receiving department.

"Gratitude is the birth of receiving."
—Joe Dispenza

Gratitude is what softens and opens the heart to receive well. Without it, there can be no receiving. A bitter heart and distrusting spirit towards people will block the receiving energy of love and healing, even though they are readily available. Shame is another state that closes the heart, which we addressed under the *"morality"* category of our money blocks exercises. Whenever you do not fully accept a gift or take a compliment, you block the energy that is flowing towards you. Since energy is energy, when you block a compliment, you are also blocking money flow! 😳

If you are ready to receive more abundance in your bank account, you also have to be willing to receive the other blessings that flow your way. The next time that someone offers to help you with something, don't brush them off. Instead say, "Thank you. I am very grateful to receive your help,".

Every time that you force yourself to receive, you will get better at it. It will continue to feel more natural. It has amazing cyclic effects, as well. The better you get at receiving, the more nourished you will become. The more nourished you become, the more love you will be able to experience. The more love you are able to experience, the more your vibration will raise. And that will ultimately lead you to expand your capacity so that you can *give more*.

The antidote to a bitter heart is forgiveness. Bitterness, resentment and rage (whether silent or loud) are defense mechanisms signaling that the heart is suffering. It is imperative to nourish the heart, to remind her that she's safe to love and trust once again. Lack of forgiveness generates very low frequencies that lead to stagnation. The longer it festers, the more stagnation forms. When you don't forgive, an opening to receive is simply not available. And if there is no opening to receive, money will have no place to flow towards.

Until forgiveness is given, money will continually be blocked. This can be a great motivator to dig deep and forgive your parents, your ex-lovers, your boss, your friends, your spouse, or anyone else that has hurt you in your past. It has cost you in huge ways. Not only in the form of heartache, but your health, wealth, and the ability to access your gifts. If you find yourself being "offended" often, this is a solid indicator that forgiveness needs to be a regular part of your self-care practice.

Money is an energetic connection that can only come through people. How you feel about others will be reflected in your finances. Those who have a hard time connecting with others, struggle with being vulnerable and open, lack trust in humanity, and regularly judge and excessively criticize others, have *major* struggles in their personal financial situations.

I want to offer you the gift of releasing resentment and offering forgiveness. I want you to experience how it feels to have your heart nourished and open to receive. I want to enable you to expand your level of gratitude to new heights! This will make it easier for you to receive money, raise your prices or ask for a higher wage, promote yourself in your business, share your heart in your community, and deepen the connection with your spouse. A shift like this changes everything!

Providing value to others by solving their problems requires emotional maturity. If you are embarking on an entrepreneurial journey, it is even *more* imperative to work on your spiritual/emotional health! Your income only grows as much as you do.

Whole Heart Protocol

Cardamom: This essential oil calms the liver and soothes irritability. The liver produces anger and rage. Cardamom also curbs excessive judgment and criticism towards people.

Helichrysum: This essential oil is a true superstar. It is the ultimate forgiveness oil, as it repairs broken hearts that have experienced betrayal and dissapointment. It sutures and dissipates the rawness of the pain so the heart has the opportunity to heal and move on. Radical forgiveness is one of the most important practices for evolving into higher consciousness. The ability to forgive and let go is an attribute of someone who has been freed from their ego rather than enslaved by it.

Rose: Since cardamom and helichrysum have calmed and soothed the body's emotional responses, the powerful benefits of rose will be able to be maximized. The unconditional love that rose provides will be able to be truly experienced by a heart that has released its pent up resentment from past traumas. Like a dry, thirsty plant soaks up water, the heart soaks up the frequency that only rose can provide. It is the oil of ultimate self-love and self-acceptance. Rose reminds us that we are worthy and deserving of love and support. It will also increase your intuition so that you can

Whole Heart Protocol

1. *Cardamom*: APPLY TO BOTH SIDES OF LIVER 14, (ALONG THE BRA LINE)

2. *Helichrysum*: APPLY TO REN 17 (ON THE STERNUM)

3. *Rose*: APPLY TO THE INSIDE OF THE WRIST CREASES

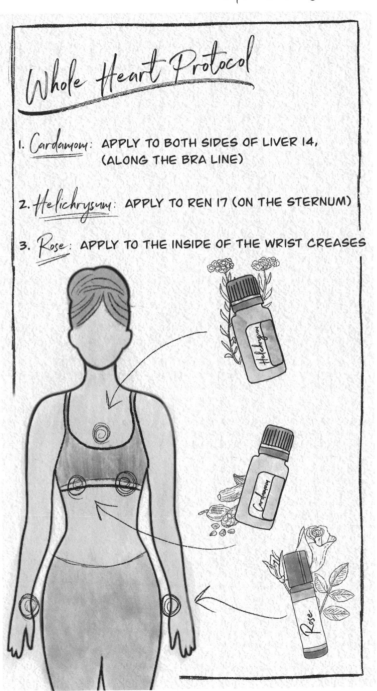

have discernment in knowing who/what we should allow in. Rose will work to prevent us from rejecting that which is good for us, as we so often do.

I am so excited to hear about all of the nourishing things you have started because you have begun to listen to and honor your needs/wants! Will you share them with us through social media? Use the hashtag **#iammagnetic** on the social media platform of your choosing, along with the changes you've personally experienced. Breaking out of old molds can be challenging! Everyone needs encouragement to regularly live in alignment with their truth.

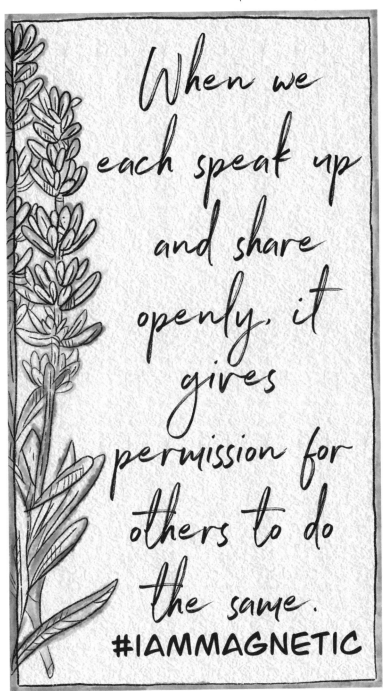

When we each speak up and share openly, it gives permission for others to do the same.
#IAMMAGNETIC

[CHAPTER 9]

I am Magnetic

Wow! You should be so proud to have dedicated yourself to making it through the entire journey of *I am Magnetic*. You, my friend, are truly exceptional. Thank you for investing time in your transformation and for allowing us to be a part of your journey. I know it hasn't been all *unicorns and rainbows*. Just as the withdrawls from a sugar-detox can make for an unpleasant experience, releasing shame and scarcity have similar effects. Your patience and dedication have empowered you through the roughest moments. As a result, you have officially shed the old version of yourself.

You are now more vibrant and the world can experience more of the love that radiates out from you. Best of all, you now get to discover how magical life truly is. Prayers get answered, opportunities appear, unexpected friendships form, ideas develop into reality, and you even experience closure from aspects of your life that have dragged on for way too long. Welcome to a life of momentum and expansion!

The combination of *Clarity*, *Flow* and *Rhythm* form the secret sauce. Each area needs to be considered in order to attract the circumstances, people, projects and resources that you desire. This isn't just a *money* story. It's a story about your life!

You have *way* more control than you think. Most people choose not to believe that, and operate their lives accordingly. They fear change; and as a result they never take the time to learn how to change their energy patterns and take accountability for their lives. Yet, they catgeorize themselves as "normal". It is *normal* to live a life filled with unnecessary suffering, chaos, stagnation and destruction. Sorry, but that's just not my style. It's no longer yours, either. You know how to change your energy patterns! You are a part of the weird and wild ones who are willing to learn new skills, put essential oils on our bodies in strange places and do non-conventional things to continually break *out* of the norm! Successful people do weird things. 😎 Be bold in color and adventurous in design. *Paint your heart out!*

After completing each chapter in this book, you are ready to take on the *I am Magnetic* blend. Every step of clearing, nourishing and harmonizing has prepared you to receive the maximum benefits of this blend. It is designed to carry forward the progress you have made in previous chapters.

Warning: Do not use this blend if you have not completed the protocols and exercises in this book! If your energy patterns are not changed before using this blend, it may exacerbate your existing money/life issues. For example, if you struggle with a severe scarcity mindset, utilizing this blend will intensify those feelings. The blend is designed to attract more of the vibrational patterns that you emenate. Please honor yourself enough to ensure you are in the right frame of mind. The last thing we want is for you to become a magnet for chaos and destruction.

The *I am Magnetic* blend is subtle, yet powerful. It embodies *Clarity*, *Flow* and *Rhythm* all together. This blend increases feelings of worthiness, brings you in alignment with your core values, opens the heart to receive and gives courage to move forward on what is necessary. Think of it like an all-in-one blend to make your dreams come true!

One side effect I have noticed is *giddiness* upon application. Euphoria and peace envelop you for a few minutes, and then it's go time! I can't wait for you to experience it. You deserve it!

I am Magnetic Blend

Alchemy Instructions: Please add the oils in the order in which it is written. After putting in the drops of essential oils, swirl the mixture around for a minute. Then fill in the rest of the bottle with Fractionated Coconut Oil.

Location: Apply along the spine of the foot reflexology area. You should roll it up and down the area. You can then follow that with applying the blend to any other location you desire. This is a great time to *trust in your intuition!*

Frequency: Apply 2x per day. If you consider yourself an empath or hypersensitive, do not apply past 5pm (assuming you're on a day-shift schedule and need to sleep at

I am Magnetic
10 ML BLEND

65 DROPS *Magnolia* (USE A PIPETTE)

8 DROPS *Clary Sage*

6 DROPS *Bergamot*

3 DROPS *Douglas Fir*

2 DROPS *Helichrysum*

3 DROPS *Ylang Ylang*

3 DROPS *Eucalyptus*

3 DROPS *Patchouli*

1 DROP *Cinnamon*

3 DROPS *Green Mandarin*

THE "*I am Magnetic*" BLEND APPLICATION POINT

Spinal Point

RIGHT SOLE   LEFT SOLE

MEDIAL VIEW

Spinal Point

night). Sometimes, Clary Sage can be stimulating to a hypersensitive. If you feel too much momentum, you can reduce the frequency to once per day.

Length of Usage: Recommended for one month, but can be used longer.

Safety Precautions: Bergamot is a citrus essential oil that is known to be photosensitive. If you plan on being out in the sun, do not apply on an area that will be exposed. Bergamot combined with the sun rays will cause the skin to darken. The bottoms of the feet are a safe application point for days in which sun exposure can't be avoided.

Magnolia: This is a powerful essential oil with a multitude of properties. It nourishes and opens the heart to receive love, connection and healing. It helps you to embrace your divine beauty and your own worth. Magnolia also encourages you to acknowledge the life you desire and feel deserving of the miracles that align for you. Throughout this book, you have done so much up-leveling! Magnolia can help it to stay activated, in the same way that a setting spray helps a make-up artist. Applying it at the end ensures that the make-up, or in this case, the up-leveling, stays intact.

Clary Sage: This essential oil gives you insight into your life's big picture. It makes sure that your decisions and plans are in agreement with your core values.

Bergamot + Douglas Fir: These will boost your confidence and trust in yourself. Together, they invigorate the spirit to move forward with ideas and projects that have

have been put on the shelf due to fear and doubt.

Helichrysum: This is our signature forgiveness essential oil. If any regret or frustration come up in your journey, Helichrysum will be there to soothe the soul of self-deprecation.

Ylang Ylang: This essential oil will fuel your curiosity to try new things. You have to try something new in order to create something new. Ylang Ylang mitigates hesitation and unleashes your child-like spirit. Kids believe that anything is possible for them. If they want to be an astronaut, they don't list all of the logical reasons why they cannot. They spend their time learning and exploring, consumed by curiosity. Ylang Ylang reawakens this spirit within you.

Eucalyptus + Patchouli: These oils are utilized merely for harmonizing. They tie the blend together, integrating all of its functions and distributing the blend all over the body upon application.

Cinnamon + Green Mandarin: These essential oils also have the function of harmonizing, but with an extra punch. Together, they ignite a desire to share your gifts with others. They rid you of the doubt and low self-esteem that has stopped you from speaking your truth. It's the "Here I come, world! Nothing is stopping me, now..." combination.

It's time to celebrate! May you feel liberated from the shackles of hopelessness, fear, doubt, indecision, frustration and sorrow. The I am Magnetic blend takes the potential energy that has been stored in your spirit and releases it into motion! Many unexpected benefits may come from using this blend. For me personally, I noticed that I gained discipline in my eating habits! Saying no to foods that cause inflammation in my body has become easier. Alonto has experienced an increase in his productivity-level. These results were not what we anticipated. But we are so grateful!

Now it's your turn! Go out there and solve a problem that is near and dear to your heart. Pay attention to what your soul is commissioning you to do. Know that making money is a noble and positive endeavor.

Making more money means:

+ YOU ARE SOLVING PROBLEMS FOR MANY.
+ You are uplifting more people.
+ You wholeheartedly believe in yourself.
+ **YOU RESPECT YOURSELF.**
+ You are committed, dedicated and disciplined.
+ YOU BECAME A MASTER AT YOUR GIFTS.
+ Your capacity to love and serve has expanded.
+ YOU KNOW HOW TO FORGIVE AND TRUST.
+ You know how to take a vision and bring it into reality
+ YOU ARE RESOURCEFUL AND CREATIVE.

→ You inspire. ←

Will you help us to change the conversation around money? Can you imagine a world that associates those positive beliefs with wealth-creation and entrepreneurship? It begins with us! The steps we take to improve our money makeup will be felt by those around us. Our changes radiate out to others and it is inevitable that someone will want to join you in this endeavor.

Thank you for pioneering the way towards healthy money conversations. Remember to share your **#iammagnetic** story with us on social media! We are eternally grateful for your participation.

Love,

Desiree and Alonto

Let's Continue Working Together!

Our time doesn't have to end here! If you would like to continue to work with me, visit my website:

www.desireemangandog.com

There are many ways to dive deeper into your journey:

- *I am Fabulous* **BOOK:** Improve your emotional well-being with 45 essential oil recipes

- *I am Worthy* **BOOK:** Do you feel like you are not good enough? This book dives deep into releasing shame out of your heart, and embracing your beauty with total self-acceptance. Own your infinite worth!

- *Awake Yourself* **COURSE:** Shed limiting beliefs in your conscious and subconscious mind that are preventing you from greatness. This course is a *must* to create lasting changes for your mental, emotional and spiritual growth.

- **PRIVATE SESSIONS:** Get customized essential oil protocols, based on your needs, in a private session with me, Desiree. I can identify your root causes of imbalance and walk you through a protocol during the session, as well as customize a program to last you three months.

- **LIVE EVENTS:** Hear us speak at a live event or webinar. For upcoming events, check-out www.desireemangandog.com/events

You can also find me on *Facebook*, *Instagram* and *YouTube*, where Alonto and I post free content.

Facebook:

www.facebook.com/DesireeFabulousMangandog

Instagram: @desireemangandog

YouTube: www.youtube.com/desireemangandog

APPLICATION POINT REFERENCES

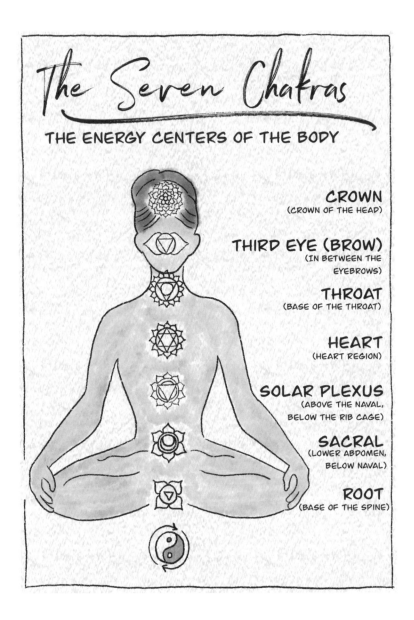

The Seven Chakras

THE ENERGY CENTERS OF THE BODY

CROWN
(CROWN OF THE HEAD)

THIRD EYE (BROW)
(IN BETWEEN THE EYEBROWS)

THROAT
(BASE OF THE THROAT)

HEART
(HEART REGION)

SOLAR PLEXUS
(ABOVE THE NAVAL, BELOW THE RIB CAGE)

SACRAL
(LOWER ABDOMEN, BELOW NAVAL)

ROOT
(BASE OF THE SPINE)

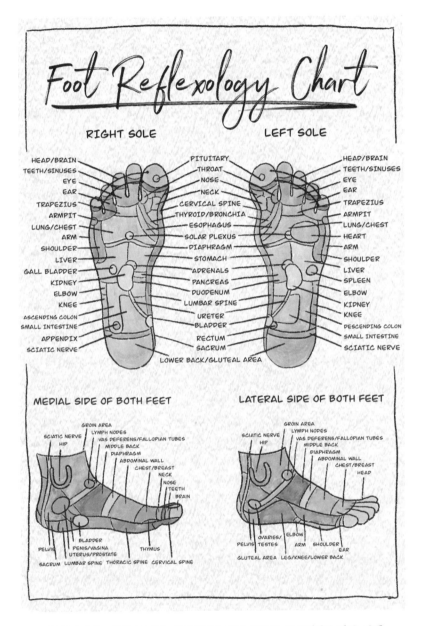

Foot Reflexology Chart

RIGHT SOLE

- HEAD/BRAIN
- TEETH/SINUSES
- EYE
- EAR
- TRAPEZIUS
- ARMPIT
- LUNG/CHEST
- ARM
- SHOULDER
- LIVER
- GALL BLADDER
- KIDNEY
- ELBOW
- KNEE
- ASCENDING COLON
- SMALL INTESTINE
- APPENDIX
- SCIATIC NERVE

(CENTER)

- PITUITARY
- THROAT
- NOSE
- NECK
- CERVICAL SPINE
- THYROID/BRONCHIA
- ESOPHAGUS
- SOLAR PLEXUS
- DIAPHRAGM
- STOMACH
- ADRENALS
- PANCREAS
- DUODENUM
- LUMBAR SPINE
- URETER
- BLADDER
- RECTUM
- SACRUM
- LOWER BACK/GLUTEAL AREA

LEFT SOLE

- HEAD/BRAIN
- TEETH/SINUSES
- EYE
- EAR
- TRAPEZIUS
- ARMPIT
- LUNG/CHEST
- HEART
- ARM
- SHOULDER
- LIVER
- SPLEEN
- ELBOW
- KIDNEY
- KNEE
- DESCENDING COLON
- SMALL INTESTINE
- SCIATIC NERVE

MEDIAL SIDE OF BOTH FEET

- SCIATIC NERVE
- HIP
- GROIN AREA
- LYMPH NODES
- VAS DEFERENS/FALLOPIAN TUBES
- MIDDLE BACK
- DIAPHRAGM
- ABDOMINAL WALL
- CHEST/BREAST
- NECK
- NOSE
- TEETH
- BRAIN
- BLADDER
- PELVIS
- PENIS/VAGINA
- UTERUS/PROSTATE
- THYMUS
- SACRUM
- LUMBAR SPINE
- THORACIC SPINE
- CERVICAL SPINE

LATERAL SIDE OF BOTH FEET

- SCIATIC NERVE
- HIP
- GROIN AREA
- LYMPH NODES
- VAS DEFERENS/FALLOPIAN TUBES
- MIDDLE BACK
- DIAPHRAGM
- ABDOMINAL WALL
- CHEST/BREAST
- HEAD
- PELVIS
- OVARIES/TESTES
- ELBOW
- ARM
- SHOULDER
- EAR
- GLUTEAL AREA
- LEG/KNEE/LOWER BACK

THIS IS WHY WE APPLY ON THE BOTTOMS OF THE FEET! LOOK AT ALL OF THE AREAS THAT GET ACCESSED BECAUSE OF IT!

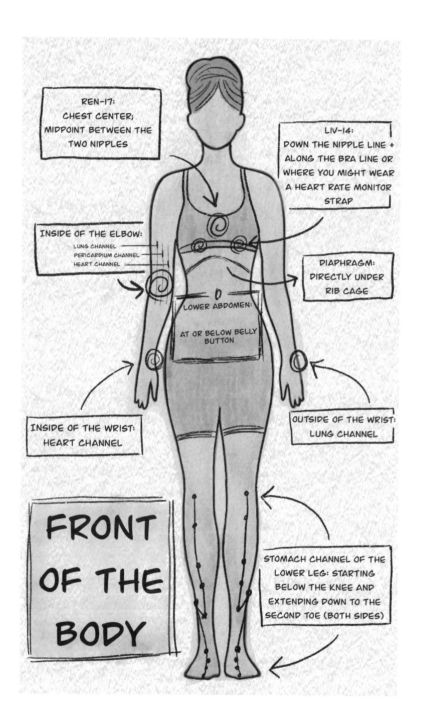

REN-17:
CHEST CENTER;
MIDPOINT BETWEEN THE
TWO NIPPLES

LIV-14:
DOWN THE NIPPLE LINE +
ALONG THE BRA LINE OR
WHERE YOU MIGHT WEAR
A HEART RATE MONITOR
STRAP

INSIDE OF THE ELBOW:
LUNG CHANNEL
PERICARDIUM CHANNEL
HEART CHANNEL

DIAPHRAGM:
DIRECTLY UNDER
RIB CAGE

LOWER ABDOMEN:
AT OR BELOW BELLY
BUTTON

INSIDE OF THE WRIST:
HEART CHANNEL

OUTSIDE OF THE WRIST:
LUNG CHANNEL

FRONT
OF THE
BODY

STOMACH CHANNEL OF THE
LOWER LEG: STARTING
BELOW THE KNEE AND
EXTENDING DOWN TO THE
SECOND TOE (BOTH SIDES)

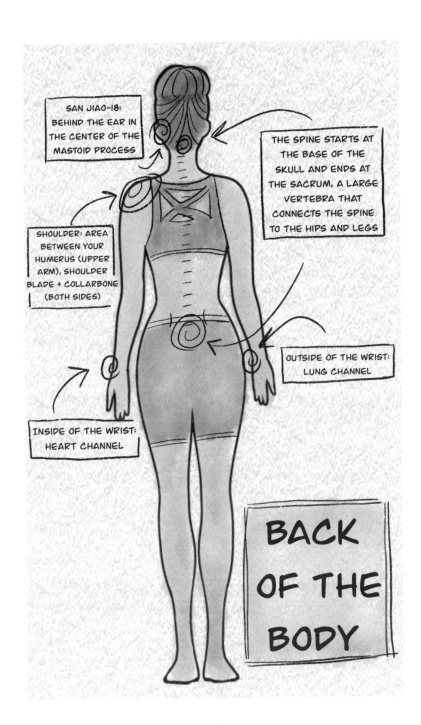

Bibliography

Deadman, Mazin Al-Khafaji, & Baker. *A Manual of Acupuncture.* East Sussex, England: Journal of Chinese Medicine Publications, 1998.

Worsley, J.R. *The Five Elements and the Officials.* Taos: Redwing Book Company, 2000.